B

BOUCHERON
Paris

cabochon
saphir.

cristal de
roche

OR

- Saphir
3 gaudrons.
OR

6

parfum
bijou

# ARRESTING DESIGN

Editorial coordination: Virginie Leroux
Designers: Julie Mattei and Magali Peretti for Pink Fluo
Translation from the French by Alison Culliford
Translation edited by Matthew Clarke


This work is printed on the registered products and brands of the Arjowiggins group:
Pop'Set, Absolut mat, Sensation tactile and Maine gloss.


© 2006, Éditions Scala

This English edition first published in 2006 by Éditions Scala
Passage Lhomme - 26 rue de Charonne - 75011 Paris
www.editionsscala.com
ISBN : 2 86656 384 0
Diffusion - Distribution : CDE - SODIS

Distributed in the UK by Scala Publishers Ltd
Northburgh House - 10 Northburgh Street - London EC1V 0AT, UK
www.scalapublishers.com
10 9 8 7 6 5 4 3 2 1

Distributed in the USA & Canada by Antique Collectors Club
www.antique-acc.com

First published in French by Éditions Scala

ALAIN LACHARTRE

# ARRESTING DESIGN
## Illustration in the Marketplace

With Françoise Aveline

*Preface by Philippe Starck*

ÉDITIONS
SCALA

# CONTENTS

Ph. STARCK    by    myself © AL.
                                    1996

"Is painting a major art and illustration a minor one?"

Like an abscess, this thorny question hurts when you touch it but, if left untreated, it can gnaw away at our enfeebled minds.

The doctor's advice is always to treat the abscess first.
So, while you argue it out among yourselves, may I offer the hazy beginnings of an answer?

Firstly, I've looked, consulted, searched, scanned what I find around me, and I've examined Lachartre's top 60.
What I found is strange but it provides some clues.
Strangely, at the end of the day, there are more good painters than good illustrators… Maybe because illustration is more difficult or more rigorous, or maybe because it demands other qualities?
Possibly.
… But I can see that a lot is left unsaid in and around illustration.

Is an art more important because its purpose is humble? Is an art noble because it is at the service of others?
Can an art based on renunciation be free of self-contempt?
A self-effacing art.
An art that is unusual because is it not egotistical, an art that speaks of what is said and not of who is saying it.
A human art which skips the pointless and sometimes obscene phase of admiration to go directly to feeling and emotion.

I could go on – "But, doctor, what about the abscess?"
The doctor replies with two observations:
    One: I've already given you an answer.
    Two: Who cares anyway?

In any case, long live the artists! We salute you.

Philippe Starck

**I** love drawing, the transfer of impulses from the brain to the hand that holds the pencil, the brush or the mouse. I love pen against paper, the smell of ink, the finger rubbing the pencil lead on the page to create a halo around the line. I love the simplicity of drawing, the face-to-face contact with a white page.

I love the artists: they are adventurers in image, who boldly go, alone, to reach their goal. To work with them is a great joy, born of understanding and mutual esteem. You only work well with those who feel you respect them, who appreciate the confidence you have in them. You are their interlocutor, and your attitude will have an impact on their work; their sensibility will be heightened, so you must not leave them in doubt. You also have to know how to listen, because illustration has its own laws. Things that you might think achievable can turn out otherwise, and only the artists know the limits of feasibility.

The starting point for every collaborative venture between drawing and public relations is that a brand wants to be heard. To speak to consumers, it develops a strategy and an advertising plan of attack. It chooses the appropriate media – television, press, posters – and devises messages, the more original and distinctive the better. In this way, the brand reinforces its recognition, enriches its image and increases the desirability of its products.

In parallel to this path, a brand must approach other targets to reinforce and optimise this strategy: journalists and opinion makers, all the links in the distribution chain, contacts who might give recommendations, not to mention the company's internal teams.

This type of communication is sometimes the most important of all, as when regulations limit the ways in which a firm can approach the consumer – in France, this is the case with champagne, for example.

This "parallel" communication is done differently, by methods that we call "non-media", belonging most often to the world of publishing: gift-books, brand or company brochures, presentation booklets for products and press kits accompanying a launch or another event. These tools do not have the ephemeral character of the advertising media; they are addressed or personally presented to the recipient and must create a privileged link between him or her and the brand. This is not mass communication but a confidential conversation between the brand and its chosen intermediaries. The care lavished on the form of an object has never had more importance; the manner in which the message is to be presented has a decisive influence on its content. This type of communication establishes a relationship akin to seduction between the sender and the receiver, who is flattered to be the recipient of a real present.

The advertising media use photography almost exclusively to reflect a target audience or their aspirations – which come down to the same thing. Drawing, however, – if it is perfectly mastered – represents a major trump card for what could be called "public-relations publishing". Why? Whether spellbinding or funny, poetic or caustic, illustration offers a personal and subjective vision that has a strong effect on readers; it summons up their childhood memories and, as a consequence, makes them more receptive to the message. Each illustrator has a signature style, a personal touch. Faced with a wealth of possibilities, it can be difficult to decide who would be the best interpreter of a brand or company and give the most fitting response to the problem in question.

It is emotion that makes us remember things. Illustration speaks directly to our sensibility, provokes our astonishment and creates echoes of our own nostalgia. The collaboration between an art director and an illustrator demands a shared vision. Both committed to the same journey, they work in tandem and share the same ambition: to astonish and captivate.

In the world of public relations, the approaches to photography and drawing are entirely different. The photographer, in a conductor-like role, imposes his vision on an entire team: stylist, models, hairdresser, assistants, etc. The work is mapped out during pre-production meetings. There is some room for artistic manoeuvre but, nevertheless, everything is demarcated "under control". The interested parties, from both the advertising agency and the client company, are kept fully informed about what is going on and are often present on the day of the shoot.

In contrast, illustrators work alone. Using their style and imagination, their lines and colours, they bring to life their vision of the message to be conveyed. Mistakes are not permitted; the client must feel at ease in the bespoke suit that is being made for him or her. This aspect of total delegation can be seen as a risk: an entire project is in the hands of a single person! It is our job to be there to answer for its success or failure. Artistic direction is essential: artists must be set on the right track, but also given plenty of freedom so that they can give it their best shot.

When a public relations project is conceived, all the means of expression are considered. The thickness and texture of the paper, whether it is smooth, coarse or transparent, warm or cold to touch – all these form part of our concerns. And the images? They must be thought up at the same time, because the whole project must move forward as one: the concept, the words, the visuals, the form, the materials… The ideas must bounce against each other, come together and grow. The client is first presented with a provisional outline. This is precise in its appearance and in the expression of the concept that has already been chosen, and it is accompanied by our recommendation for an illustrator. The outline contains rough sketches showing our intentions but, alongside, we also present some examples of the chosen style. Whether the artist is known or unknown, what counts is talent, the capacity to breathe life into an idea. We have discussions from this first stage onwards, to involve the artist very early on in the progress of the work. His or her point of view is important, providing fresh input that can help us improve the project.

The "home-made" sketches in the outline are a perilous exercise. They have to be sufficiently clear to express the ideas, but remain as simple outlines so as not to constrain the artist. Their value is as a platform: for our client, who supports our proposals, and for the illustrator, too, for whom they serve as a guide. The artist must enjoy our unconditional support: he or she is the best, the only one to be able to bring this project to life, like an actor chosen by a film director on the basis of sensitivity and talent… Of course, the recommendation takes into account the projected target. If the chosen illustrator is published in the press read by the target audience, its memory will be stirred and this can give rise to a collaboration.

Outlines, tracings, sketches… the art director's job has really started. There are regular discussions with the illustrator – by telephone, fax and e-mail – punctuated by meetings. The important thing is to keep the momentum going. Showing the client the state of play is an important moment – perhaps he or she needs reassurance; above all, the client must not be left in the dark, after having trusted your choices and taken them on board. At a certain stage in the progress of the work, it is enjoyable to organise a meeting between the client and the illustrator. Curiously, such exchanges rarely happen, as if there were a fear of upsetting illustrators by inviting them to come out of the ivory tower of their studio. However, these meetings allow each party to put a face to a name: people perform best when they know who they are working for.

Children's book illustrators, press cartoonists and comic-book authors have all, at one time or another, contributed to the business of brand promotion – for our greater pleasure.

As professionals who are passionate about their art, art directors have the job of convincing them to take part…

Alain Lachartre

**P**erfume stimulates a part of our brains in touch with our most intimate selves. It can evoke memories, throw us into a state of agitation and awaken our sensuality. Like music, perfume has its own language. Cosmetics are the informers in the world of beauty. They plant touches of colour to attract the glance of others to whatever we choose to highlight.

Working like a metaphor, illustration allows one to recreate the stream of impressions that perfume arouses. Like perfume, it has the capacity to transport us and make us dream; or, playful and quirky, to take us by surprise. In confidential tones, it reminds us with a cheeky remark that seduction is only a game.

Une odeur de mystère, où domine le santal...
Le noir complet, puis, un beau jour, l'éclat somptueux de la fête...
Qui sort de l'ombre ?

Le 23 avril 1990
à 21 H.

TOUT A COMMENCÉ EN MARS 1986 dans un des laboratoires les plus secrets du monde. Après des mois et des mois de mise au point, le produit était enfin prêt. On savait pour qui : un homme hors du commun. Il fut habillé de noir souligné de blanc, dans le plus pur respect des traditions de la maison. Mais tout pour lui devait être différent. Déjà unique par son nom, ÉGOÏSTE serait unique en tout. Plus tard, on décida qu'il serait révélé le 23 avril 1990 et les meilleurs talents se mirent au travail...

Jacques TARDI
**Chanel**
1990 – *Egoïste* the fragrance

## Me, myself and I

A motorbike tearing through the night in a film by Jean Cocteau or Fellini; a drawing in black, grey and white; a murky, crepuscular light: it was with this sober press pack, in October 1990, that international journalists first encountered Chanel's new fragrance for men, *Egoïste*.

In the extremely codified world of perfume promotion nothing like this had ever been seen before! Once again, Chanel had decided to spring a surprise. Jacques Helleu, who is responsible for projecting the company's image, had previously hired Jean-Paul Goude to make an advertising film that had stuck in everyone's memory: at each window in the facade of a luxury hotel, a model in a Chanel evening dress hurls imprecations – in time with the rhythm of the shutters that she flings open and shut – at an egoist, of whom we see nothing but the hand.

For this new fragrance, Jacques Helleu mentioned the possibility of commissioning a comic book. Knowing of our work with illustrators and of the recent book *Objectif Pub*, the Public Relations Director approached us with the project and then entrusted us with it. We showed various maquettes to Jacques Helleu: one of them grabbed his

DÈS JANVIER, le 18 exactement, Chanel rassembla sa force de vente internationale, une grande famille de 700 personnes. Le lendemain même, tout le monde était prêt à l'action. Ensuite, les présentations se succédèrent dans 17 pays, regroupant plus de 5 000 professionnels.

LE JOUR J SE PRÉPARA DANS TOUTE L'EUROPE. Pour ce lancement, plus de six millions d'échantillons et deux millions de produits furent fabriqués. Une flotte de camions fut prévue pour les acheminer à temps. Le 23 avril 1990 au matin, les vitrines de plus de 5 000 parfumeries d'Europe devaient être entièrement consacrées à ÉGOÏSTE, avec un décor d'une rare élégance, mais qui ne pourrait pas passer inaperçu. Après l'Europe, le reste du monde suivrait.

PENDANT LE MOIS D'AVRIL, la presse publia de mystérieux messages : un "JE" dont le sens devait aussi être révélé le Jour J : c'est le mot qui compte le plus pour l'ÉGOÏSTE.

ÉGOÏSTE de Chanel, tout en restant très secret, entra dans l'univers des médias. Dans toute l'Europe, 300 pages lui furent réservées, et plus de 15 000 abribus portèrent sa griffe.

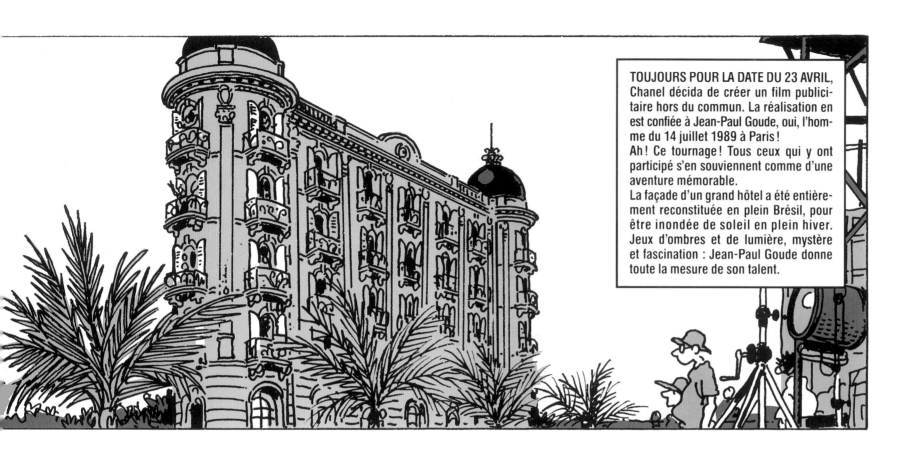

TOUJOURS POUR LA DATE DU 23 AVRIL, Chanel décida de créer un film publicitaire hors du commun. La réalisation en est confiée à Jean-Paul Goude, oui, l'homme du 14 juillet 1989 à Paris!
Ah! Ce tournage! Tous ceux qui y ont participé s'en souviennent comme d'une aventure mémorable.
La façade d'un grand hôtel a été entièrement reconstituée en plein Brésil, pour être inondée de soleil en plein hiver.
Jeux d'ombres et de lumière, mystère et fascination : Jean-Paul Goude donne toute la mesure de son talent.

!? DRRiiiNNG

LE JOUR J, SUR TF1 : un film de 52 minutes sur "La règle du JE" consacré à l'égoïsme, valeur éternelle et phénomène de société. Le thème est traité avec humour et séduction. Une seule coupure publicitaire dans cette soirée, réservée bien sûr à la première diffusion du film publicitaire, programmé pour plus de 500 passages en Europe. L'émission sera ensuite adaptée et diffusée sur les principales chaînes de télévision européennes.

Depuis janvier, l'ÉGOÏSTE invitait les journalistes dans son appartement. A Neuilly, à Madrid, à Milan et dans d'autres villes d'Europe. Des limousines venaient les chercher et en chemin une cassette leur présentait cet homme si mystérieux. Ils découvraient ensuite son décor, ses objets, le raffinement de son environnement. Pour approcher la vérité de l'ÉGOÏSTE, cette visite valait toutes les conférences de presse du monde.

JE SAVAIS QUE TOUT SERAIT PARFAIT !

LE 23 AVRIL 1990 A 21 HEURES, DES MOTARDS LIVRENT UN PRÉCIEUX FLACON A QUELQUES MILLIERS D'ÉGOÏSTES PRIVILÉGIÉS EN EUROPE. LE SUCCÈS, DÉJÀ.

Réalisation : VUE SUR LA VILLE, textes : Nicole CONTENCIN, dessins : Jacques TARDI

attention, and he put forward the idea that it should be Tardi who carried it out. The latter had just published his adaptation of Céline's book *Journey to the End of the Night* for the publisher Gallimard-Futuropolis.

Tardi was attracted by the idea of a motorcyclist crossing the city full pelt at a fixed time of night to deliver a bottle of the new Chanel fragrance to the favoured few, so we went to see Jacques Helleu together. We had to climb to the fourth floor of the Chanel offices, where we found a white carpet and a slight scent in the air… Tardi's old raincoat and rather eccentric appearance looked incongruous in this temple of luxury. Elegant and impeccable as always, Jacques Helleu came to greet us. He offered his hand in welcome and said to Tardi, quite simply: "I have so much admiration for you". They went on to talk about old locomotives, a shared passion. All in all, it was a wonderful meeting.

Once the scenario was finished, we hesitated over the technique to adopt for the black, grey and white drawing: grease pencil with medium tints, or pen and ink with full-tone shading? In the end, the second solution won the day, as it was cleaner, more direct, and perfectly in tune with the traditions of Chanel.

Philippe CARON
**Chanel**
1991 - *Couleurs et Lumière*
Yellow

## The colours of Chanel

Advertising for the major cosmetic brands essentially involves providing information about the products over the course of the seasons, which are themselves governed by launches and new products. In 1991, the Chanel make-up creators, Dominique Moncourtois and Heidi Morawetz, joined forces with the Public Relations Department and decided to approach the press in a different way. Their aim was to position Chanel as *the* specialist in colour. The idea was to offer journalists a timeless reference tool, both attractive and useful, that would serve as a glossary of colour in all its forms, as well as providing editors with a data bank where they could find ideas for talking about colour in new ways. The project was ambitious, for Chanel sought to create a work that would make its mark and, by association, establish links with the beauty, richness and variety of the colours in its own range of make-up.

We were given *carte blanche* to bring the project to a successful conclusion. Our ideas and proposals were refined over the course of exchanges with our contacts

*Couleurs et Lumière · 3*

*Couleurs et Lumière · 4*

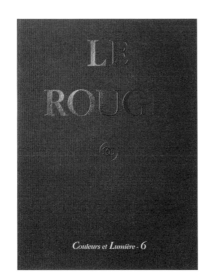

*Couleurs et Lumière · 5*

*Couleurs et Lumière · 6*

at Chanel. The result was six large-format albums, united under the title *Couleurs et Lumière* (Colours and Light), each one devoted to the exploration of a colour – Yellow, White, Black, Blue, Green and Red – approached from various angles. Each work was published in a print run of two thousand copies in various languages: French, English, German, Italian, Spanish and Japanese. We adopted the principle of a succession of double pages, a full page of text facing an image, alternating with a strongly visual double-page with a photo in the centre. The texts were entrusted to specialists – historians, scientists, writers – under the supervision of Nicole Contencin. We had total freedom to propose the content and treatment of the images, as well as to choose the artists, photographers and illustrators. The difficulty was in finding enough new material in the themes to create surprise and enticement around each colour. The albums were to be sent out one after the other over the course of two years, and we had to provoke enough interest to create a real effect of anticipation.

The project resulted in some memorable work sessions, which brought together all the authors concerned. In the Yellow album, the semiologist Bernard Dahan decoded the language of the colour in everyday objects.

1. Philippe CARON
**Chanel**
1991 - *Couleurs et Lumière*
Yellow

2. Jean-Claude GÖTTING
**Chanel**
1991 - *Couleurs et Lumière*
Yellow

1

2

1

2

1. BENOIT
**Chanel**
1992 - *Couleurs et Lumière*
Red

2. Emmanuel PIERRE
**Chanel**
1992 - *Couleurs et Lumière*
Red

3. FLOC'H
**Chanel**
1992 - *Couleurs et Lumière*
Red

In the hands of Jean-Philippe Delhomme, tennis balls, New York taxi cabs or a "yellow submarine" took on the acid colours of modernity – and a small yellow Post-It with the Chanel logo was stuck by hand to each copy of the album. A short story by Lyndon Wolff told an original tale of transgression – the crossing of a yellow line on a mountain road – that ends in disaster. Jean-Claude Götting illustrated this with a drawing of a strip of black asphalt hugging dark rocks on the edge of a cliff. The use of oil pastels gives the scene a dramatic depth. A thin, pale yellow line winds through the heart of the image, issuing a deceptively low-key warning. To conjure up yellow in art, we proposed an opening in a trendy gallery: for this, Philippe Caron made sketches of celebrities, allowing readers to have fun recognising figures like Karl Lagerfeld, Woody Allen and Philippe Starck.

Like Black, White is an important colour for Chanel, as it serves as one of the bases for powders and other make-up. To get across fully the iridescent effect of the light-correcting pigments explained by Chanel's Research Director, we attached, by hand, four little sachets of face powder to an illustration by Philippe Caron, which are held in place by a sticky label with the Chanel logo.

3

Pointe Desny - 16 MARS - 9h

Munich - 27 AVRIL - 16h

Les Cyclades - 23 JUIN - 17h

1 Cape Cod - 14 OCTOBRE - 15h

Erfoud - 10 DECEMBRE - 8h

2

1. LOUSTAL
**Chanel**
1991 - *Couleurs et Lumière*
Blue

2. Philippe CARON
**Chanel**
1991 - *Couleurs et Lumière*
Blue

3. Philippe WEISBECKER
**Chanel**
1991 - *Couleurs et Lumière*
Blue

3

Ever MEULEN
**Chanel**
1992 - *Couleurs et Lumière*
Green

To accompany the historian Geneviève Leroy's account of how women down the ages have ruined and damaged their skin in search of a translucent complexion, Emmanuel Pierre produced a quirky comic strip in the style of Tarot cards. Philippe Sollers, Michel Pastoureau, François Rivière and Anne Bragance, each in their turn, made contributions as writers over the course of the two years. All the illustrators were assigned subjects suited to their particular artistic concerns. So, the great traveller Loustal was asked to show that all skies are different by painting a scene from five places in the world to illustrate "Why the Sky is Blue". And Philippe Caron's work on the theme of "Klein Blue" is truly the vision of an artist who also enjoyed playing with references to Matisse.

To create a surprise, you should never be where people expect you to be. Thus, Ever Meulen, a veritable architect of images, invented a sophisticated geometrical composition to conjure up the green of 18th-century garden rooms evoked by landscapers Sylvie Brossard and Alexandre Chemetoff. The result is totally fresh, from the expressions of the characters to the comedy of the situation in which a panic-stricken contemporary of Marie-Antoinette finds herself trapped in a maze.

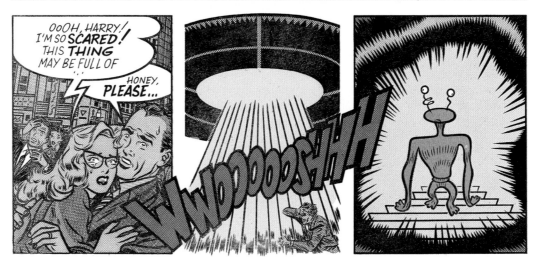

1. Walter MINUS
**Chanel**
1992 - *Couleurs et Lumière*
Green

2. Pierre LE-TAN
**Chanel**
1991 - *Couleurs et Lumière*
Blue

With Red, we enter the world of passion and seduction. When Chanel Red touches the lips, it also quickens the heart. Erotic, dynamic and energetic, it attracts wearers who feel an affinity with these qualities. An instrument and secret of female beauty, red sets off the black of a voluptuous evening gown with an indiscreet cleavage by Valérie Lancaster. With Ruben Alterio, red is heat and movement, an intrinsic state of the body and spirit revealed by clothing. And Floc'h has produced a checkerboard of icons in miniature: a Ferrari, an English telephone box and a bottle of ketchup, but also, hand-stuck to each album, an imaginary, but real-looking postage stamp bearing the image of the volcanic Gabrielle Chanel.

To give a special allure to the albums, we conceived them as artists' books, like the ones printed by the Draeger brothers in the 1930s. They were unbound, with the leaves simply folded inside a sober, coloured cover, with only the name of the colour appearing in bright lacquer with the Chanel logo.

Valérie LANCASTER
**Chanel**
1992 - *Couleurs et Lumière*
Red

Ruben ALTERIO
**Chanel**
1992 - *Couleurs et Lumière*
Red

Emmanuel PIERRE
**Chanel**
1992 - *Couleurs et Lumière*
Red

Emmanuel Pierre

# Si Coco m'était contée

*Jacques Helleu parle de Coco, de Vanessa, de Goude*

## A grown-up Wonderland

While we were immersed in the illustrations for the *Couleurs et Lumière* albums, life and creation went on at Chanel. Jean-Paul Goude had just produced for Jacques Helleu the advertising film for the *Coco* perfume, with Vanessa Paradis as a bird on a trapeze. The filming, as always in the case of Chanel, involved some spectacular sets, including a 50-ft-high golden cage in which Vanessa was perched, while releasing torrents of perfume from a giant bottle. To illustrate the press pack that accompanied the release of the film, Jacques Helleu and Jean-Paul Goude wanted to call on an illustrator who could recreate the marvellous world of the film in his own way. We talked about it together and our choice was Pierre Le-Tan, with whom we had already had the opportunity to work. To reproduce spatially the decor and scenery, we proposed a "pop-up", a 3-D image obtained by folding paper. Before we knew it, we were commissioned to undertake the project,

*Un beau jour, sur un coup de tête, Gabrielle Chanel délaissa son hôtel particulier et s'installa dans une suite du Ritz, ouvrant sur la place Vendôme.*
*Avec juste quelques objets, elle y reconstitua son univers: des paravents en laque de Coromandel, un épi de blé peint par Dali et, sur un guéridon, parmi d'autres objets offerts par le duc de Westminster, une petite cage dorée...*

Pierre LE-TAN
**Chanel**
*1991 - Coco*

Il était une fois une jeune trapéziste qui, là-haut sur son trapèze, se prenait pour un oiseau — un oiseau de paradis dans une cage dorée.

Dehors, les nuages s'amoncelaient. Au loin grondait le tonnerre. A la lueur des éclairs, l'oiseau sifflait pour se donner du courage. ..."Stormy Weather"...

Ne dit-on pas que, les soirs d'orage, les esprits reviennent visiter les lieux qu'ils ont aimés ?

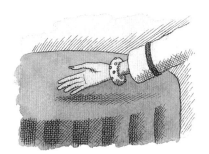

L'oiseau s'en balance. Il virevolte dans sa cage et joue avec un lourd flacon de cristal d'où s'échappe un sillage délicieusement parfumé.
Pendant ce temps, à travers les barreaux, un gros minet l'observe. Il a, pour l'oiseau, les yeux de la Bête pour la Belle.

Il était une fois un oiseau de paradis qui rêvait d'être une jeune acrobate...

39

Pierre LE-TAN
**Chanel**
1991 - *Coco*

and so came into contact with the perfectionism and professionalism of Goude. He pushed us as far as we could go to make the illustration as perfect and realistic as possible, which meant reworking with Le-Tan not only the faces of Jacques Helleu, Jean-Paul and Coco Chanel, but also the legs and feet of Vanessa Paradis, to achieve the maximum precision. To emphasise the sophistication and finesse of the lines, we chose a matt, textured, pale ivory paper. The result is a sophisticated book resembling an *objet-d'art*; handling it conveys a feeling of elegance and preciousness that reflects the spirit of the perfume. It is already a highly coveted collectors' item.

Au Ritz, à deux pas de la maison de couture de
Gabrielle Chanel, sa suite existe toujours.
Un voluptueux persan blanc aime s'y coucher sur
un guéridon, près d'un grand flacon de Coco.
Pensivement, le chat contemple l'oiseau de paradis
qui continue de le narguer dans sa cage.
Ne dit-on pas que, les soirs d'orage, les esprits
reviennent visiter les lieux qu'ils ont aimés ?
...« Stormy Weather »...

1

2

## Journeys through the imagination

Chanel's commitment to the tradition of *haute parfumerie* meant that, by the early 1990s, it was one of the last firms still to use natural raw materials to create its perfumes. Jacques Polge, the company's exclusive "nose", selects the best parts of fragrant plants from across the globe, according to the season: flowers, fruit, roots, resins… Chanel's Public Relations department, inspired by the theme "Every minute, somewhere in the world, a flower opens for Chanel", decided to send a press team – a photographer and a journalist – to gather images and atmospheric reports on the main plants used to make the perfumes. The aim was to compile a mass of material that could answer even the most searching questions of the media, as well as contributing, on an internal level, to the demands of departments like Marketing and Training. It would also serve as a support for a large promotional operation aimed at the international press, as yet undefined.

This world tour was a large-scale operation that had never been undertaken by any other perfume manufacturer or magazine, on account of the large cost involved. The project therefore generated a great deal of interest, and, by the end of the assignment, which lasted almost a year, a rich treasure trove of material had been revealed. It was a fabulous travelogue which recaptured the

environment of these plants of remote and prestigious origins, and the dreams and exoticism that surround them. The idea of producing travel diaries was proposed, but Chanel wanted something that was closer to the perfumes themselves. The journalist therefore proposed writing stories that evoked the charm of the four great women's perfumes – *No.5*, *No.19*, *Cristalle* and *Coco* – through an imaginary meeting with the flowers from which they are made.

The Chanel press office asked us to provide all this material – which was unusual to say the least – in a form consistent with the spirit of the brand. The challenge was to introduce luxury and sophistication while preserving the natural and spontaneous aspects of the documentary photos. What oniric universe should be chosen to engage visually journalists from all over the world, beyond their own cultures and imaginary worlds? The equation was not a simple one to solve, but, once again, illustration seemed to us the best way to add a creative and artistic dimension that could only enrich the work. To avoid any visual clashes with the photos, the drawings were designed to surround the text, to bring out the elements of fantasy in the stories.

We chose four illustrators whose styles seemed to be in harmony with the worlds of the various perfumes: Ruben Alterio, Daniel Maja, Loustal and Bertrand Bataille. We asked each one to produce a series of drawings of

3

4

5

6

7

8

1 and 4. Daniel MAJA
**Chanel**
1994 - *Les Contes aromatiques*
*N° 19*

2 and 5. Bertrand BATAILLE
**Chanel**
1994 - *Les Contes aromatiques*
*Coco*

3 and 6. LOUSTAL
**Chanel**
1994 - *Les Contes aromatiques*
*Cristalle*

7. Ruben ALTERIO
**Chanel**
1994 - *Les Contes aromatiques*
*N° 5*

8. Jean-Claude GÖTTING
**Chanel**
1994 - *Les Contes aromatiques*
*Antaeus*

different sizes, from vignettes to full pages, which would be used to complement the text presenting the perfume and the photos. The evocation of *No. 5* involves a story that unfurls in the south of France, in Grasse, the capital of perfumery. The tale presents an ambassadress who resembles the actress Carole Bouquet, photographed in fields of flowers wearing a wide-brimmed Chanel hat. Ruben Alterio worked with the hot colours of his palette to depict a sun-baked earth in tones of red and burnt Sienna. Carole Bouquet is suggested in silhouette, from behind, but she is recognisable by her hat.

The mime in the story dedicated to *No. 19*, a spirited perfume full of passion, inspired Daniel Maja to think of the characters of *commedia dell'arte*, who are excitable and full of movement. An acrobatic Pierrot juggles with a swirl of flowers in a pantomime that runs through the pages.

Loustal depicts Sicily and La Réunion, the two islands that meet in the story of *Cristalle*, imbued with all the spontaneity and youthfulness characteristic of this perfume. Using a rather child-like style, he sketched a volcano, a quiet corner on a boat, mermaids and shoals of multicoloured fish jumping in the sea. Finally, Bertrand Bataille conjured up for the opulent *Coco* a refined nocturnal setting where East meets West.

*Les Contes aromatiques* (Aromatic Tales) was finally presented in the form of four albums, in 33 x 24 cm landscape format, in a hardback presentation box. To introduce the natural theme, the covers were designed with shades of beige and almond green. The albums were bound with a skein of raffia. Each work was introduced by a photo under a sheet of tracing paper, on which the title of the story is printed. The other photos appeared before and after the illustrated tale, in a full-page spread, on gloss paper that enhances light and contrasts.

*Contes aromatiques*, which was translated into several languages, received a very positive response from journalists — so much so that the Public Relations department decided to adapt them to a smaller format and offer them as gifts to customers in Chanel boutiques. We produced a 13 x 18 cm edition, on matt paper, still in landscape format, keeping a synopsis of the text, the illustrations and two photos. Two new stories, for fragrances for men, have now expanded the collection. The illustrations adopted a black-and-white treatment with one complementary colour, chosen by Jacques Helleu to go with the packaging for each perfume. *Antaeus*, an extrovert scent inspired by mythological references, was coupled with the powerful lines of Jean-Claude Götting's architectural drawings, with their strong emotional intensity. And it was Tardi, already responsible for the press pack for *Égoïste*, who illustrated the tale dedicated to *Égoïste Platinum*, a fresh fragrance glowing with energy.

Max CABANES
**Chanel**
1997 - *Le Conte de Noël*

## A Christmas of lacquer and gold

A Christmas story provided the opportunity for Chanel to present seasonal good wishes to the press. The idea was to create a precious, sophisticated book around the text, so that the recipient would discover the message in a similar way as opening a present. By using the symbolic colours of the brand – black and white – along with gold, the traditions of Chanel and of Christmas itself would be combined. A soft case with four flaps unfolds to reveal the story. Max Cabanes' illustrations play on shades running from black to white. The use of gold to represent the halo of the stars, a flower or wafts of perfume floating up to the sky highlight elements of magic, creating an effect like a jewellery box. Each of the illustrations could in itself be a Christmas card.

For the outside of the case and the cover of the story book, we chose a lightly brushed matt gold, with plenty of density. The shiny black of the box's interior recalls the lacquer reflections that Gabrielle Chanel loved so much.

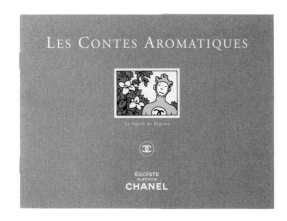

### Platinum Sun
*by Françoise Aveline*

*A spaceship glided like a silent liner through intergalactic space. The passengers standing in the panorama room watched the stars whirling past. Their eyes, once bright with hope, now reflected nothing but distress and resignation. They could not remember how long they had been searching for the Platinum Sun which had suddenly stopped shining on their planet. They had sailed through nebulas, dodged meteors and were now wondering where to go next. Their civilization was 10,000 years old and had long since resolved any problems of survival, but now they were gripped by a different fear. Without the precious light of the Platinum Sun, their powers of imagination would rapidly degenerate. Once plunged into deep depression, they would be powerless to stop the gradual, inevitable destruction of their advanced human cells.*

*The head of the interplanetary mission was a young man, elected for his intelligence and open mind. Generous and enterprising, a man of action, he had long ago chosen to serve those around him. Born under the sign of the White Sun, he was called PLATINUM.*

*The engines had slowed down. Pessimism had set in on board the spaceship. For some time now, PLATINUM had been keeping himself to himself. Rumour whispered that he was turning away from the group and becoming more and more selfish. Doubt began to seep in. At last, one morning, after a particularly sultry night, PLATINUM appeared and called the Council of the Wise. His weary face seemed more relaxed, as if relieved. A hush fell over the council as he began to speak:*

*— I have spent a great deal of time working lately and you have seen little of me. Perhaps you even thought that I was losing interest in the community: if you did, you do not know me well enough. But my research was crucial and demanded my whole attention. If I have neglected you, it was for your own good. His listeners stirred, puzzled by his words.*

*— Two things have emerged from my work. The first is bad news: we will never find the Platinum Sun. It imploded thousands of years ago and I am now certain that its light has been lost forever.*

*Cries of horror greeted his statement, but he went on:*

*— I also have some good news: a reasonable distance away is a small planet called Earth, where living organisms have developed under the rays of another sun which has similar effects on the imagination as the Platinum Sun. Earthlings call them wood, moss, flowers, resin… All we have to do is to find them and capture their essences. When we breathe them in, our imagination will be instantly reactivated. His listeners rose in a group and applauded. PLATINUM was carried in triumph on their shoulders. Joy spread throughout the spaceship as everyone raced back to their workstations to set the expedition on a course for Earth.*

*Some time later, the planet on which their hopes were set was spotted through the panoramic window. According to PLATINUM's calculations, they should approach a minute island in the southern hemisphere. The technicians disengaged a spaceship small enough to land anywhere; PLATINUM chose two companions and, with cheers ringing in his ears, he set off for Earth.*

*The ship touched down on Reunion Island. PLATINUM marvelled at what he saw, but was not surprised, for his intelligence circuits, linked up to the immense Universal Knowledge data base, had long since told him what he would find there. He immediately recognized the geranium, whose precious essence is concealed in its silken stalks. Then, their ultrafast ship raced them to Haiti to dig out vetiver roots, to Paraguay to gather orange tree leaves and*

Jacques TARDI
**Chanel**
1994 - *Les Contes aromatiques*
*Égoïste Platinum*

to the East for galbanum. Speeding over Africa to Europe, they plucked cedar from the Atlas mountains, rock-roses in Andalusia, lavender and rosemary in Provence.

During his long hours of solitary labour, PLATINUM had learnt how to make the plants yield up their powers of imagination. He extracted, distilled and blended essences and fragrances. Absorbed by his creation, he did not notice his companions slip away. Soon the moon rose. PLATINUM kept watch all night long, alert to the slightest sound. Finally, in the morning, he saw his friends in the distance, covered in confusion.

– Don't be angry, one implored. We knew that our mission was nearly over and we did not want to give up everything we had discovered on Earth, the fragrances, the colours, the quivering air.

– And then, his companion went on, last night we realised that our behaviour was really too…

– Selfish, perhaps? suggested PLATINUM airily with a glint of amusement. The runaways hung their heads. Then PLATINUM handed them a bottle.

– What do you think of this composition? Don't you think it contains everything that prompted you to selfishness?

– Yes it does! It's incredible! cried the first.

– It will save the imagination of those who are waiting for us. We will call this perfume EGOISTE as a reminder of your temptation, but that will remain our secret.

– PLATINUM EGOISTE, corrected the other, with mingled enthusiasm and relief.

– If you insist, smiled the young man. But now it is time to leave. We will soon have an opportunity to prove that selfishness sometimes masks generosity.

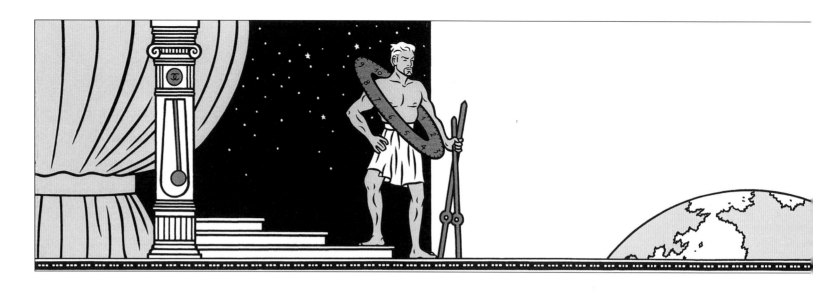

## Ode to a Grecian urn

A few years later, Chanel launched *Allure*. This new perfume for women combined the timeless aspect of the brand with a pioneering new composition squarely aimed at the future. The illustration for the story was inspired by the decoration of Ancient Greek vases, whose colour palette was adapted by Jacques Helleu for the perfume: black, white, gold, and a special tone of beige, tinted with the delicate pink of a woman's skin. Having secured the services of Walter Minus as the artist for this project, we explored all sorts of possi-

bilities before coming up with the idea of expressing timelessness — the unique quality of *Allure* in the story — through simple figures with black forms.

The final image was only achieved after many trials and tribulations on the graphic front. Traditionally, the figures are seen from behind, seeming to be moving towards a radiant future, but Chanel maintained that they should be viewed from the front. This frontal portrayal meant that we had to find the most appropriate angle that allowed us to still suggest a dimension of infinity. In the end, Walter Minus produced a beautiful piece of work that was extremely silhouetted and theatrical.

Walter MINUS
**Chanel**
1996 - *Le Conte Allure*

### A Tale of Time Present
*by Françoise Aveline*

*There is an implacable god who has been with us since
the beginning of the world: Chronos, the God of Time.
Guardian of eternity, he inflicts on the living the weight
of the days which pass without hope of return.
In these times, he is aware of a confused fear which seems
to rise from distant humanity on the eve of the Third
Millennium. He remembers the great fear of the year 1000
and the strange behaviour it created among men.
Once again, men feel lost: they do not know where true
values lie, they bubble with enthusiasm at the slightest*

*pretext for ideas, fashions and their fellow men,
and as quickly drop them again.
Foolishly, to forget the power of Chronos, men have
turned to the Goddesses of Time Present. Bursting with
pride at the importance they are accorded by humanity,
the Goddesses are nevertheless worried. They know that
unless they manage to persuade Chronos to allow them
to accompany him to the kingdom of the Eternal, they are
condemned. With little time left, they decide to request
an audience.
The first to present herself is Youth. Bravely she begins to
speak, without hesitation:*

IZAK
**Chanel**
*1996 - Le Petit Livre beige*

— *Thou, Master of Time, thou knowest well the nature of men. Thou knowest how much they venerate me, how sad they are when I leave them. To give them reassurance, allow me to stay in eternity.*

*But Chronos sends her away with these words:*

— *Youth, thy reign is short, and Men must accept this. Thou art not eternal and there is nothing I can do for thee.*

*Next comes Beauty:*

— *Look at me, Chronos, and see how desirable I am. In the world, Men have invented a thousand ornaments to subjugate me and keep me with them. Help me to satisfy their dreams and carry me into eternity.*

*But Chronos turns away:*

— *Thou art as beautiful as a flower, and like a flower thou art doomed to fade. Thou art not eternal. I can do nothing for thee.*

*Then comes Fashion, dressed in the latest modern finery. Chronos expresses annoyance:*

— *Dost thou not remember that thou art here for a short time only? What dost thou want of me?*

*Finally, Riches approaches, glittering with eyecatching brilliance, but Chronos stops her:*

— *Doubtless thou thinkest to obtain all thy desires, but Time cannot be bought ! And he chases them off with contempt, exclaiming:*

— *Away with you all. Not one of you can resist the passage of Time.*

*Then the god notices that one goddess has asked for nothing. With her casual ease and natural elegance, she displays an indefinable grace.*

*Although vexed by the little attention she has paid him, Chronos asks her name:*

— *Allure, she replies, serenely.*

*Captivated, the god insists:*

— *Where hast thou found the confidence to be so simply thyself?*

*Allure smiles and holds out a bottle:*

— *Here is my spirit. Every woman who can capture it will discover the truth that is within herself. For Allure has a multitude of faces. She does not need beauty, she is indifferent to riches and cares nothing for fashion. The quality of Allure comes from within.*

— *Come close beside me, says Chronos.*

*Thy place is in Eternity, since thy essence is inexhaustible. The woman who possesses it will travel the world, free and self-assured, with the long stride of those who, like thee, can defy time.*

*Then Chronos walks slowly away, to the rhythm of the heavy pendulum which has not ceased for an instant to mark time. As a breath of perfume spreads over the earth, his steps become softer and then are no longer.*

IZAK
**Chanel**
*1996 - Le Petit Livre beige*

52

## Le Petit Livre beige

*Allure* marked a total break with traditional perfume formulae. Jacques Polge created a scent with six facets that express themselves in a different key on each woman, thus allowing her to reveal her own personality. To accompany the press launch, we came up with *Le Petit Livre beige* (Little Beige Book). Unlike Chairman Mao's *Little Red Book*, it invited women to break the diktats of fashion in order to rediscover their own personal allure. For the first time, a product was defining its identity among women through difference and personality rather than through beauty.

Izak seemed the right man for the job. His chic characters create a spontaneous bond and complicity with
readers. Izak's women remind us all of someone, giving
us the impression that we have met them somewhere
before. "*In fact Izak lives in a world of women. He has
four sisters and the majority of those whom he calls
his heroines resemble his sister Isabelle,*" explains his
agent, Virginie Chalamel. For *Le Petit Livre beige*, we
devised playlets where women behave just as in real life,
with their audacity, their doubts and their little foibles.
Izak's humorous approach worked wonders.

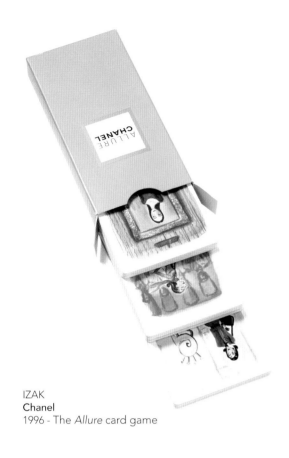

IZAK
**Chanel**
1996 - The *Allure* card game

ELLE A UN CÔTÉ FÉLIN

ELLE A QUELQUE
CHOSE DE SOLAIRE

ELLE NE CALCULE RIEN

## An alluring hand

Because there are 36 ways to have allure, we also invented a "Game of Six Families" to introduce the six facets of the perfume: woody, timelessly floral, fresh, imaginatively floral, oriental and fruity. Each one is composed of six cards offering a possible definition of allure. It is played like the game of patience, each player building up their ideal of allure by juxtaposing a card from each facet. To bring this game to life, we had to think up funny or moving situations corresponding to each definition. Izak set his long-legged heroines against watercolour backgrounds of six different colours. He claims to treasure "fabulous" memories of this collaboration. It also gave ideas to a number of competitors, who made him offers which he had the decency to refuse.

ELLE EST
D'UNE GRÂCE INFINIE

ELLE SAIT TOUJOURS
TROUVER LE TON JUSTE

ELLE RÉINVENTE LE
CLASSIQUE

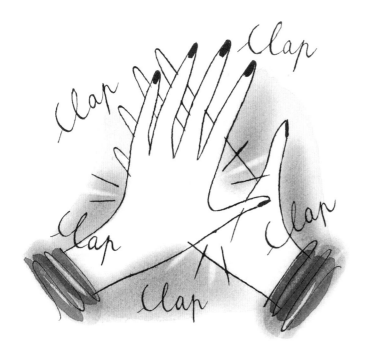

## Caught red-handed

Beauty is a serious business but it is sometimes good to treat it lightly. To accompany the launch of a new collection of Chanel nail polishes, we decided to appeal to journalists with a game, in a proposal that was both playful and sophisticated.

We explored all the visual and conceptual ways in which we can play with hands, and make hands play for us. As always, a message was hidden in the game. The art of reading palms and the language of gestures are depicted, along with an anthology of Chanel nail polishes, in the guise of collages, cut-outs, coded messages and 3-D images. The free hand extended to us by the press office allowed us to be extremely creative. The most difficult part was finding a graphic style for portraying hands that was suited to Chanel. It had to combine clarity of line, simplicity, elegance and wit. After several trials and proposals to Jacques Helleu – who had imagined something in the style of Lichtenstein – we finally decided to commission the illustrations for *Jeux de mains* (Play of Hands) from Cyril Cabry, who used a highly stylised line with no effects of relief. This booklet received the Club of Art Directors' Prize for the Best European Publication in Dublin in 1996. Later, using the same principle, we produced *Rires et Sourires* (Laughter and Smiles) with Cabry for the launch of a new range of lipsticks.

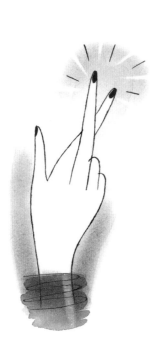

Cyril CABRY
**Chanel**
1995 - *Jeux de mains*
and *Rires et Sourires*

Dites-moi,
vous ne seriez pas
du type bilieux rétracté tonique,
avec une tendance schizoïde ?
En tout cas,
vous jouez du piano...

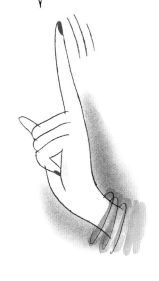
Pas vraiment,
je suis violoncelliste
et je vis un bonheur
parfait.

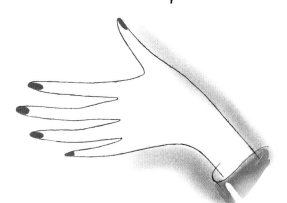
Tout le monde
peut se tromper...

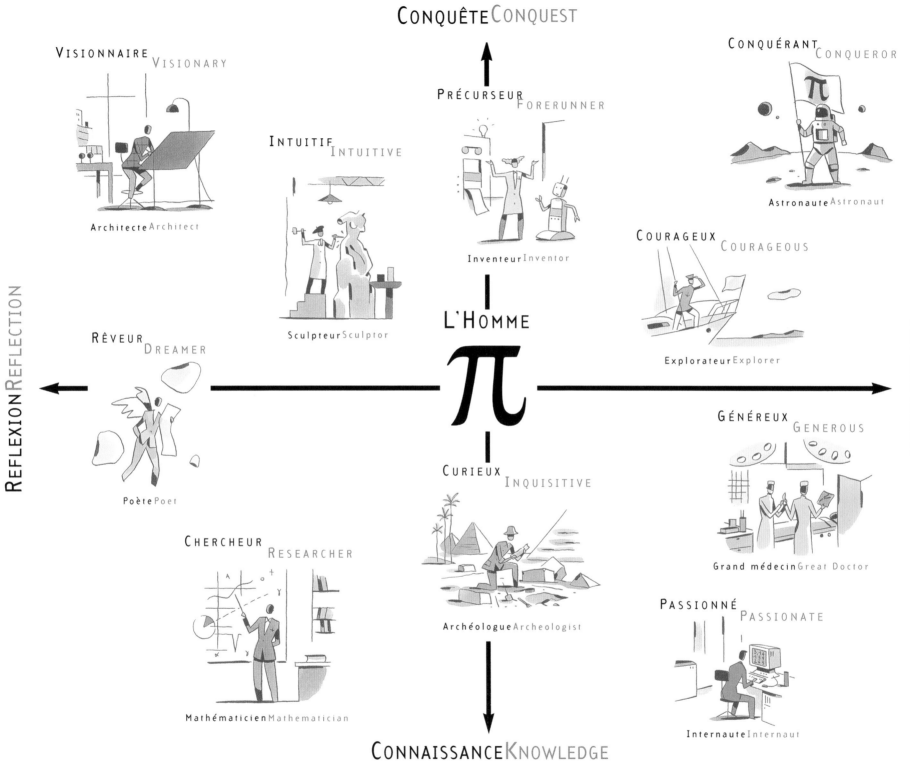

CONQUÊTECONQUEST

VISIONNAIRE VISIONARY

ArchitecteArchitect

INTUITIF INTUITIVE

SculpteurSculptor

PRÉCURSEUR FORERUNNER

InventeurInventor

CONQUÉRANT CONQUEROR

AstronauteAstronaut

COURAGEUX COURAGEOUS

ExplorateurExplorer

REFLEXIONREFLECTION

RÊVEUR DREAMER

PoètePoet

L'HOMME

π

ACTIONAction

GÉNÉREUX GENEROUS

Grand médecinGreat Doctor

CHERCHEUR RESEARCHER

MathématicienMathematician

CURIEUX INQUISITIVE

ArchéologueArcheologist

PASSIONNÉ PASSIONATE

InternauteInternaut

CONNAISSANCEKNOWLEDGE

CARLOTTA
**Givenchy**
1990 - *Hot Couture*

François AVRIL
**Givenchy**
1990 - $\pi$

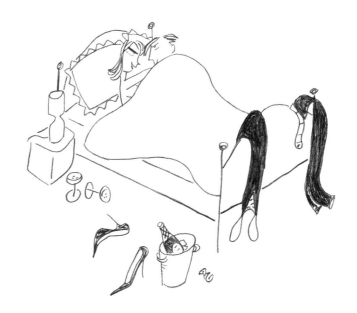

## Infinitely likeable

The art of designing a press pack or marketing dossier for the launch of a perfume means first of all knowing how to interpret a concept in a few carefully chosen words. With $\pi$, Givenchy created a masculine fragrance for modern-day heroes. $\pi$ is the unattainable number, the symbol of a perpetual quest for infinity. We devised a "map" that placed the $\pi$ man at the centre of himself and the universe, between thought and action, conquest and knowledge. François Avril's illustrations portrayed men who exceed their limits every day by merely doing their job.

In the case of *Hot Couture*, the illustration had to convey the spirit of the perfume, which is carefree, sexy, sparkling and extremely feminine. Carlotta's flower-women are immediately likeable and recognisable. The lively brushstrokes have a touch of spring about them, along with the colours and lightness of raspberry champagne.

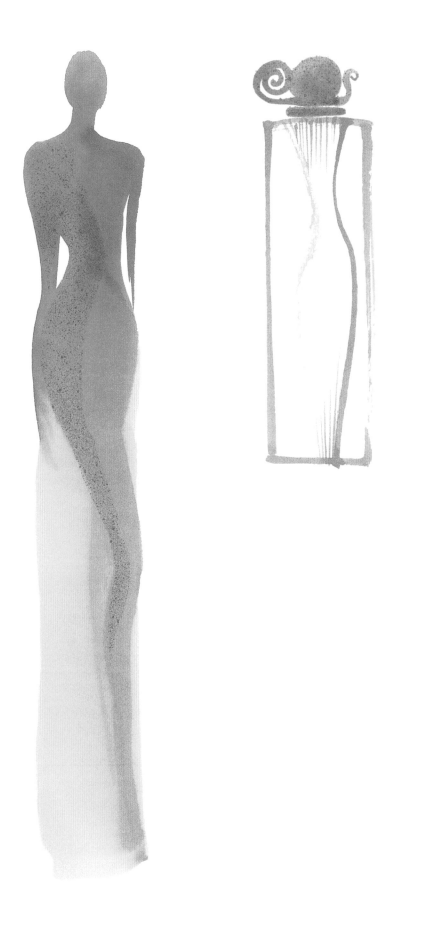

## Seduction in silhouette

Organza is a silk fabric that is so fine and fluid it is almost invisible. It is also the name of a feminine perfume by Givenchy that "deifies" the eternal female and highlights its mythical dimension. The bottle evokes classical statuary through its use of drapery and gold. To launch the Scintillante collection, *Organza*'s line of beauty products for the body, we designed a 40-cm-long vertical folder for the press pack, which was closed with a flap that suggested the lines of a woman's body. Aurore de la Morinerie's brushstrokes blend the bodily and the immaterial in the idealised and inaccessible silhouette of a woman, dressed in the wafts of her fragrance like a halo of organza.

Each of the products in the line is evoked by a sketch of a gesture, highlighted by a shimmering shower of gold. The depiction of each sparsely suggested body part puts the accent on sensation and allows it to preserve all its mystery. To add to the sense of refinement, each illustration is protected by a film of tracing paper, providing a glimpse of what lies beneath.

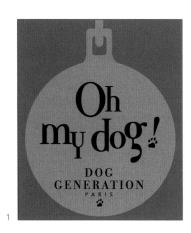

## Why dogs and cats are lapping it up

At the beginning of the 21st century, a new trend exploded in the USA: canine luxury. Thirty-six million American dogs receive a Christmas present each year. In New York, 300,000 dog owners each spend 10,000 dollars a year on their pet. Laurent Jugeau and Etienne de Swardt, at that time in charge of development in the Marketing department of Parfums Givenchy, were convinced that this growing infatuation of man for animal could open up a new international market. With Olivier Echaudemaison, the artistic director of Guerlain, they created *Dog Generation*, the first brand of high-end products and services for dogs.

To establish the brand, they decided to launch the first luxury perfume for dogs, to be sold in a selective network of outlets, and they entrusted us with the design of the press pack. Revolutionary and new, militant and assertive, Oh My Dog! was intended to captivate dog owners who wanted to give their pet the very best. The tone of the press pack had to be sophisticated, even a little snobbish, while also tapping into the emotional appeal of friendship between man and animal. It was written in three languages – French, English and Japanese – and so had to be culturally meaningful all over the world. Anja Krœncke produced the illustrations. Her style, which borders on design and is streaked

with an almost imperceptible wry humour, allowed us to create a universal setting that could equally be taken for the Bois de Boulogne or New York's Central Park, near her own home. She brought a sophisticated and exclusive dimension to the relationship between owner and dog by sketching a fashionable apartment decorated in very contemporary colours.

Later on, Dog Generation launched Oh, My Cat!, a perfume for cats, using an approach that placed the emphasis on feelings. We were looking for different atmospheres in the images and a different image of the animal's owner. The illustrations by Walter Minus referred back to the cartoons of the 1960s and established an

affectionate and humorous setting. The characters, in the style of the comic books of that era, are simple and likeable when seen in the company of their beloved pets. The atmosphere makes a strong appeal to tenderness and evokes a feeling of happiness and innocence – which is of course inherent to cats themselves.

Walter MINUS
**Dog Generation**
2001 - *Oh My Cat!*
Press pack

F lavours lead us on a voyage through the world of the senses, an exploration of all the variations on the sin of gluttony. Which style is most suited to the depiction of a gleaming sardine, a bubbly champagne or a fleshy fruit? How do we convey freshness, suggest a harvest atmosphere or evoke a distant country of origin?

Illustrators already know how to reinvent colours that speak to the taste buds. It is up to us to know how to link their world with that of certain food outlets; to convince the artist that that the potential customer will recognise themselves in a particular image. Our job is to dare, guide, instil confidence, for the ultimate aim is, as always, to surprise.

*Previous page:*

Jean-Yves DUHOO
**La Grande Épicerie de Paris**
*2004 - Escales*

## Flavours and colours, from home and abroad

In 1990, the agency CLM BBDO was in charge of the Monoprix account. Bruno Le Moult and Pascal Manry, the creative directors, asked us to develop some small-format catalogues to be distributed at store entrances to present the Monoprix Gourmet range of products. The produce itself would be photographed in *Le Guide Gastronomique des Terroirs* (The Gourmet's Guide to the Land), but the spirit of the country and the regions, and the brochure itself, was to be conveyed through illustration, which had to establish an atmosphere that was personal and mouth-watering. Loustal came to mind, and he broadened the scope of his work by using oil pastels. This sensual, earthy medium added a delicious smoothness and a gentle but realist thickness that seemed to stimulate the sense of taste.

Loustal, who had just published his first *Travel Diary*, is a peerless colourist, and pastels gave him the means to use light to great effect and create evocative images of great intensity.

LOUSTAL
**Monoprix**
1990 - *Le Guide Gastronomique des Terroirs*

His bright, dense colours were juxtaposed in contrasts highlighted by the use of a black outline that contained, finished and defined each element in the composition. Beyond the overall attractiveness of the picture, the viewer was invited to appreciate, one by one, the roundness of each apple, the fleshiness of an artichoke and the succulence of roast beef tied up with string. Loustal is a creator of atmospheres, accustomed to telling stories in a series of boxes, but here he took us even further in a single image. By showing us salmon laid out in front of a window overlooking the sea, reflecting the colours of a sunset, he told us a story: the end of a day's fishing in Scotland. The fisherman has taken off his boots and his cap. The catch was good and he is satisfied – time for a little whisky! And the reader-consumer starts to get hungry! The same went for the coffee, picked amidst lush vegetation suggesting a land that is pure and bountiful. The cleanness of the man's clothes, the precision of his movements and even his slightly enigmatic expression evoked a precious product that must be treated with care, its intense aroma seemingly embodied in the scorching glare of the sun. Like postcards, Loustal's illustrations depicted flavours from abroad and offered emotions based on tastes that made us dream of travelling to faraway lands.

Isabelle DERVAUX
**Monoprix**
1990 - *Le Plaisir du frais*

## Freshness, an instruction manual

To mark the introduction by Monoprix of the *puce fraîcheur*, a device that allowed customers to check the freshness of the products in its stores, the company produced a small information booklet for free distribution. A real instruction manual, *Le Plaisir du frais* (The Pleasure of Freshness) was above all an educational tool that explained how the freshness chip works, reminded readers of the importance of keeping food at the right temperature and advised them how to buy, conserve and consume fresh produce. The aim of the illustration was to lighten up the subject by injecting simplicity and humour, as well as encouraging consumers to see themselves positively as resourceful people endowed with common sense.

Isabelle Dervaux, who originally came to our notice through some small cards published in Japan,

Comment Fonctionne la Puce Fraîcheur?

# Qui dit Frais dit Froid

La température joue un rôle capital dans le maintien de la fraîcheur : le froid permet aux produits de vieillir moins vite. Les vitamines vivent plus longtemps, les principes nutritifs sont plus actifs. Le froid ralentit aussi l'altération des produits. Utilisé de façon durable et continue, sur un produit sain, il maintient constante sa qualité.

le PLAISIR du FRAIS

MONOPRIX LANCE
LA PUCE FRAÎCHEUR
Une innovation dans l'art de bien se nourrir

had been recommended to us by Philippe Arnaud, her agent in Paris. Her minimalist, very feminine style, with its heightened simplicity, creates dynamism tinged with humour. The consumer can identify with this healthy, slightly starry-eyed woman who takes the busy life of a young mother in her stride, with a smile on her face. Working between Paris and New York is child's play nowadays, thanks to the Internet, but this was not the case in 1990. Isabelle's drawings had to be dispatched by air. As we were often working against the clock, we established a schedule with her: the packages were left at 5pm at the FedEx office near her home, and arrived at our Paris office, in the Marais, at 11am the following morning – an eighteen-hour trip, door to door. Her parcels still had a whiff of Manhattan about them. At that time, these "lightning" methods made us feel as if we ruled the world.

1 and 5. Cyril CABRY
2. DUPUY & BERBÉRIAN
3. Jean-Claude GÖTTING
4. Philippe PETIT-ROULET
**Monoprix**
1991 - *Le Plus Monoprix des Monoprix est à Neuilly*

## A little secret between friends

In 1991, the Monoprix Sablons store reopened after a complete refurbishment. Situated in Neuilly, one of the smartest neighbourhoods in western Paris, it was to be the spearhead for a move towards a more up-market positioning on the part of certain large stores. This was a chance for Monoprix to speak to its customers, adopting the tone of neighbours passing on a good tip, to attract their attention to the new look of the store. The illustration had to convey chic elegance and demonstrate that Monoprix and its customers had the same values and the same sense of the "art of living". In its brochure *Le Plus Monoprix des Monoprix est à Neuilly* (The Ultimate Monoprix is in Neuilly), various themes were tackled – the store's architecture, layout, design, food, prices and services – each illustrated by a full-page drawing. To show the diversity on offer, we called on eight different illustrators, including Philippe Petit-Roulet, Jean-Claude Götting, Dupuy & Berbérian, Philippe Caron and Cyril Cabry. Each one created a setting and lovingly peopled it with characters representing the store's clientele, using a light, even cheeky touch, as if to say, "Here we are among friends, in a store that was made for us".

– "Il ne faudra pas oublier les radis."

"Le plaisir d'acheter commence par le plaisir de flâner."

"Tiens, les voilà!"

## Tasteful, whatever the tone

The Grande Épicerie de Paris is a magical place. With its windows along rue de Sèvres, on the Left Bank, this section of the Bon Marché is a temple to up-market gastronomy, dedicated to the impossible-to-find product. It is a meeting place for connoisseurs, culinary stylists and knowledgeable enthusiasts. It is a feel-good place, akin to an art gallery. There is nowhere else like it in all of Paris.

When Frédéric Verbrugghe took over the management of Bon Marché at the start of the new millennium, its food division basically used photographs for its communications. The new boss was a comic-book enthusiast who grew up on *Pilote*, and a big fan of Gotlib; already convinced of the effectiveness of illustration, he was very keen to use this medium, but he was afraid that it could be perceived as "not serious enough". In his own words, he said that he and his team had to feel sufficiently "mature" about the tone they wanted to adopt before they undertook this stimulating collaboration, which has now lasted many years.

Jean-Yves DUHOO
**La Grande Épicerie de Paris**
2004 - *Escales*

Iris de MOÜY
**La Grande Épicerie de Paris**
2005 - Christmas Catalogue

KAWAÏ !

**VODKA BELVEDERE**
Bouteille 40°,
70 cl - 44,00 €

BELVEDERE
VODKA

DISTILLED AND BOTTLED IN POLAND
BY POLMOS ŻYRARDÓW

IMPORTED

We worked out an advertising presentation based on the idea of small-format books which would be entertaining, informative and profusely illustrated. Published over the course of the year, with one appearing every two months or so, they would either be mailed out or distributed at the entrance of the store. Although there were certain unifying factors, such as the use of glossy tracing paper, we endeavoured to make each book different in terms of its shape, paper and format. So, each time we presented a new style to Françoise Flament, the Marketing Director, and her team, we enjoyed the same pleasure of seeing the surprise on their faces.

For example, in 2002, to enliven the Christmas catalogue in this advertising-heavy period, we proposed illustrating six "Left-Bank New Year's Eves" featuring typical couples with whom the store's customers could easily identify. The full-page drawing was matched with a text designed to highlight the "fashionable" aspect of the characters. We dreamt up scenarios and imagined the settings for the various situations. Anja Kroencke, whose work is regularly published in the magazine *Wallpaper\**, brought her personal touch to the settings, figures and furnishings. Her own references as a trendy young woman, a New Yorker by adoption, inform her sophisticated, finely honed style. It was a way of introducing a slightly off-beat, detached tone, and thereby imbuing the brand identity with a new look.

In 2005, another book was aimed at the same clientele but adopted a different tone: *Résolutions* was the starting point for light-hearted, creative incitements to succumb to temptation, based around a theme, a product or a specific feature of the store. We turned to the deft, knowing pen strokes of Carlotta for

Iris de MOÜY
**La Grande Épicerie de Paris**
2005 - Christmas Catalogue

François AVRIL
**La Grande Épicerie de Paris**
2003 - Store facade

Anja KROENCKE
**La Grande Épicerie de Paris**
2002 - Christmas Catalogue

Chez Julie,
réveillon "tendance".

Elle sait ce qu'il FAUT porter, ce qu'il FAUT déguster. Elle s'habille en rose quand tout le monde est encore en noir, elle "invente" le sirop barbe à papa et "relance" la confiture de roses. Chaque année, elle choisit un thème et le décline avec bonheur. Plaisir des yeux, plaisir du goût.

## Chez Carla et Luigi, viva Italia!

Ils sont parisiens d'adoption, mais ils travaillent pour une griffe de mode milanaise. Carla appelle tout le monde "chérrri", on les adore, et pour rien au monde on ne manquerait leur réveillon. Tout vient de leur pays : un sublime jambon, les antipasti parfumés d'une huile d'olive divine, les panettone moelleux… Luigi vous a-t-il montré son dernier portable?

Serge BLOCH
**La Grande Épicerie de Paris**
*2005 - Résolution n° 1 : Passer d'une rive à l'autre*

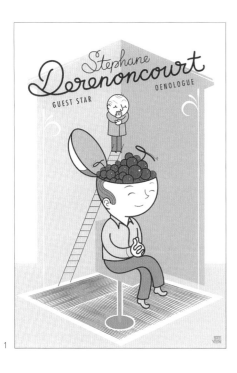

1

1. Steven BURKE
**La Grande Épicerie de Paris**
*2005 - Résolution n° 3 : Se laisser tenter*

2. CARLOTTA
**La Grande Épicerie de Paris**
*2005 - Résolution n° 2 : Faire une chocothérapie*

3. Anja KROENCKE
**La Grande Épicerie de Paris**
*2002 - Christmas Catalogue*

2

Chez Karine et Sam, les idées créatives.

Elle est céramiste, il est photographe.
Leur premier luxe : l'espace, dans leur
loft qui est une ancienne usine.
Pour eux, Noël est surtout une
occasion de recevoir les amis de toujours.
Pas de guirlandes, pas de menu traditionnel :
des découvertes, des "coups de cœur" et l'envie
de les partager. Karine ne passera pas des heures dans
la cuisine. Champagne et sushis ? Pourquoi pas.

3

the invitation to indulge in "chocotherapy". Printed in pink and chocolate brown, on a large page of glossy tracing paper folded in eight, it was intended to guide customers towards the various sections of the store in which they can eat or buy chocolate. For *Résolution n° 4 – Être une food fashion victim of the world* – the Grande Épicerie asked us to coordinate a dynamic duo: Sophie Fontanel, a columnist for *Elle* magazine, for the text, and Marie Perron for the illustration. The aim was to touch customers' most fashion-conscious points by reflecting their own customs, as filtered through the unique viewpoint of the writer.

A few months later, in the Christmas catalogue, we adopted a register that could not have been more different, with the deliciously fresh and childlike style of Iris de Moüy. This variety of forms of expression

Chez Alexandra,
élégance absolue.

Ultrachic, une allure folle ; pour elle,
la sophistication est une seconde nature.
Le décor, l'éclairage, la table... tout est
à son image : une perfection qui va de soi.
Alexandra va à l'essentiel, c'est-à-dire le
meilleur. Saumon de Norvège, caviar béluga,
champagne extra-brut... Pour elle, le goût
du luxe, c'est d'abord le goût du vrai.

constantly revitalised and enriched the project. Our objective throughout was to surprise and to create a sense of wonder, while presenting many different facets of the Grande Épicerie. "Illustration allowed us to construct an image for ourselves and, at the same time, commercially, to establish greater proximity and an emotional side to our relationship with our clientele," acknowledges Frédéric Verbrugghe. Our job was to find the tone appropriate for presenting audacious ideas without falling into caricature. The key was to know how far we could go without exceeding the limits, taking care never to lose sight of the suitability of our proposals.

Marie PERRON
La Grande Épicerie de Paris
2005 - *Résolution n° 4 : Être une food fashion victim of the world*

AU JAPON, ON EMBALLE CHAQUE FRUIT DE FAÇON RAFFINÉE...

...à la Grande Épicerie, Caroline adore l'idée.

A PARIS, SE FAIRE UN PLATEAU-COUCHE-TÔT EST DU DERNIER CRI...

...à la Grande Épicerie, Caroline digère déjà.

A LONDRES, EN CE MOMENT, LES GENS DÉGUSTENT DES INSECTES...

...à la Grande Épicerie, Caroline goûte, en toute confiance, le chocolat à la fourmi.

Pour cet été
Je Propose la véritable
Sauterelle du Togo au Gandujaaaaa...

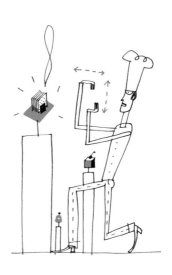

Éric GIRIAT
**La Grande Épicerie de Paris**
*2006 - Backstage*

86

## Reinventing reality

"A single quality, the best ", was the motto of the widow Clicquot, a woman far more fascinating and passionate than her respectable status could allow to be known. *À la recherche de la perfection* (In Search of Perfection) was a generic brochure destined for a large audience. In collaboration with Marie Grandcolas, the director of publications, we designed it as an itinerary around a personal world – a brand, a history, a know-how – with the festive aura associated with the company's products. Photos, still-lifes, photo-stories… these visual treatments followed one after the other and blended together, creating an impression of richness and diversity. Illustration introduced a break in the narrative, but above all it allowed us to represent a reality that never really existed.

The widow Clicquot was a timeless figure whose wine was celebrated by famous personalities, notably writers, over different periods, sometimes as much as 50 years apart. Our idea was to reunite them. It would provide information in a nutshell in a most surprising way! Floc'h drew a plush salon-library, the imaginary salon of the Veuve Clicquot, in which four elegant characters raise a toast to the portrait of madame Clicquot. They are Proust, Pushkin, Gogol and Sacha Guitry, all easily recognisable. Artistic licence allowed us to convey the message in a single glance, with a knowing touch of humour.

Illustration also allowed us to convey the romantic stature of the young woman who took the reins of her husband's business when she was widowed at the age

Emmanuel PIERRE
**Veuve Clicquot**
*1995 - À la recherche de la perfection*

of 27 and would go on to pour her entire imagination and personality into her inspired intuitions. There is no portrait of her at that age. Lorenzo Mattotti visualised her as Scarlett O'Hara in the film *Gone with the Wind* – the same courage, the same energy, the same authority. Her domain was Tara, the land of vineyards. The red dress signified a fiery temperament. The orange sky recalled adversity, the obstacles of social norms and family traditions against which the young woman had to fight. The widow Clicquot became a heroine. In contrast, Lorenzo Mattotti reinterpreted a painting that depicted her later in life, as she is remembered today. This time, white was predominant, suggesting serenity, while splashes of orange announce the symbolic colour of the brand.

How can one convey the expanse and variety of a vineyard, with its grapes ripening gently in the sun, from a single viewpoint? By firing the imagination with the charming names of the vines and local place-names such as "Vertus" and "Les Joyettes". We reinvented the *Carte du Tendre* which, in the hands of Emmanuel Pierre, owes as much to the illuminated manuscripts of the Middle Ages as to the 18th-century "Love maps" that inspired it. The transposition is surprising, flattering the cultivated reader and adding a real emotional dimension. It allowed us to inform people about the character of each of the *terroirs* in an elegant way.

## A fascinating story

In her desire for perfection, Madame Clicquot was distraught when she saw her wine clouded by deposits. In 1816, she had a flash of inspiration and invented the riddling table. When told in the style of a comic book, this somewhat technical discovery became a gripping adventure. Jean-Charles Kraehn is a specialist in historical comics; his work is precise, clear and "classical". Using a scenario by Stan Barets, he recounted the true story and gave it plenty of life by alternating general scenes with close-ups. The result is a history lesson that is fun to follow, with information that can easily be read and assimilated.

Jean-Charles KRAEHN
Veuve Clicquot
1995 - *À la recherche de la perfection*

Tinou Le JOLY SENOVILLE
**Veuve Clicquot**
*1996 - Portrait chinois*

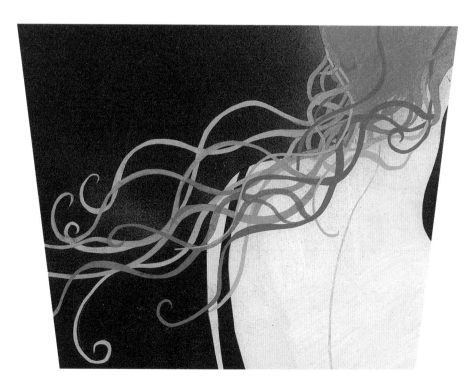

## A collage of metaphors

On 19 September 1996, Veuve Clicquot celebrated the first vintage of *La Grande Dame Rosé*. To conjure up an image to represent it, we decided to create analogies, according to the principles of a "Chinese portrait": what would it be if it was …

a place, a sky, a jewel, a woman? Tinou Le Joly Sonneville's illustrations established an atmosphere, a world of connections where the images conjured up flavours. Produced as delicate paper collages, in a harmony of pinkish, warm brown, gold and silver tones, they conveyed a subtle emotion, the quintessence of luxury.

BENOIT
**Charles Heidsieck**
2001 - *Snack Art® by Charles Heidsieck*

*– Quelle joie ce Snack Art® sur le green... Tu m'écoutes ?*

*– Cher Antoine, vous ne pensez pas que Daniel Thibault a totalement raison quand il dit
que le Brut Réserve mis en cave en 1996 a une onctuosité qui tapisse bien le palais?
– Oui, il est très épanoui.*

*– Ouiiiii Jean-Charles chéri, vous avez mille fois raison. Seule votre mère
réussit à merveille cet équilibre subtil entre le moelleux de la chair de cabillaud
et le croquant de la peau grillée caramélisée.*

*– Entre nous, qui a parlé de* Snack Art® *en premier ?*

## The sophisticated art of picnicking

Venture off the beaten track a bit, forget the classic eating rituals – this was the message of *Snack Art®*, with which Charles Heidsieck hoped to launch a new, more everyday way of drinking champagne. Inspired by the fashion for Asian titbits, *Snack Art®* was presented as a contemporary art: that of drinking champagne while elegantly nibbling at refined little mouthfuls in the most unusual circumstances.

In the launch brochure, we brought to life the unconventional aspect of this new approach by picturing little scenes in which champagne spontaneously appears, in the most unexpected circumstances. In the hands of a cartoonist, anything becomes possible. Benoît, well-known for his work with *Paris Match*, created six large images that portrayed *Snack Art®* in environments which are sophisticated but totally unexpected, such as the bridge of a ship in a storm, a golfing green or an improvised meal in a bathroom. Benoît is a surrealist poet in the tradition of his fellow Belgian, René Magritte. His images were full of freshness and absurdity. His characters were true originals, natural eccentrics. The humour came from their ability to maintain their elegance wherever they are, politely indifferent to the reality around them. This imbued them with a kind of poetry.

– *Écoutez ça... Définition du* Snack Art® : "Art de se réunir entre amis pour explorer des saveurs nouvelles, associées avec des champagnes de différentes durées de maturation en cave. Improvisation programmée, conviviale et chaleureuse."
- *Eh bien voilà, c'est tout à fait nous !*

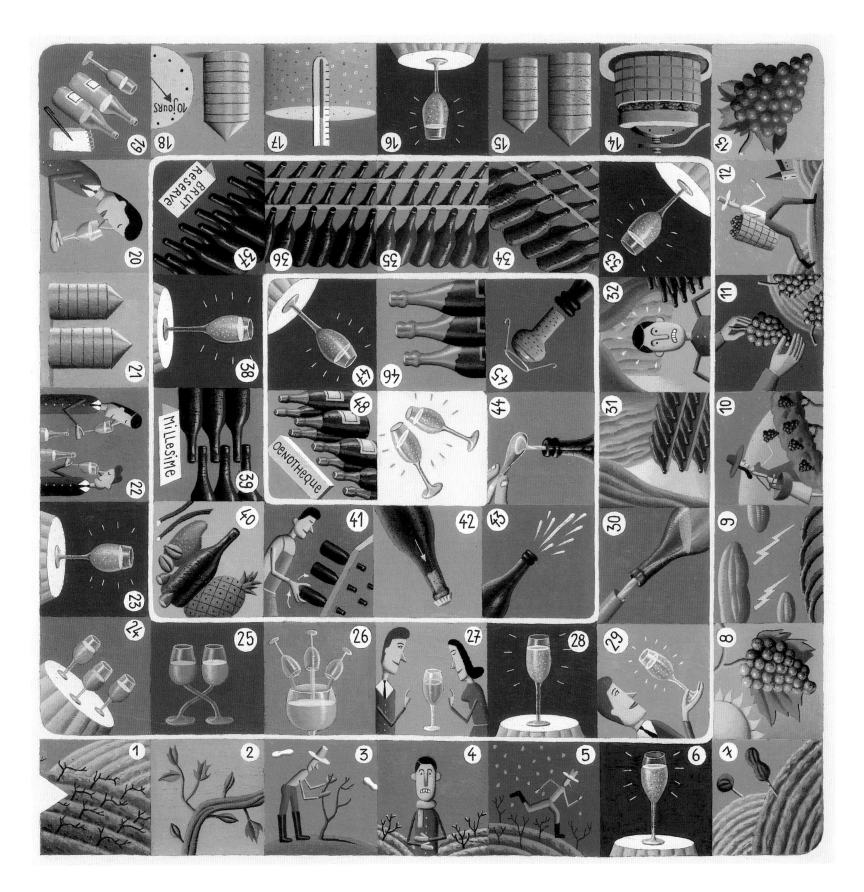

Martin JARRIE
**Charles Heidsieck**
2005 - *Le Jeu de l'oie*

Martin JARRIE
**Charles Heidsieck**
2005 - *Le Jeu des petits chevaux*


Jean-Claude GÖTTING
**Piper-Heidsieck**
1996 - *Les Moments rouges*

LOUSTAL
**ECS**
1988 - Annual report

## Games for learning

We learn better when having fun, as all children know. For Charles Heidsieck, we pushed the principle of fun-filled learning to its limit with the creation of two board games designed by Martin Jarrie.

*Le Jeu de l'oie* (The Goose Game) presented the history of champagne through 49 little squares on backgrounds of various colours. There was something childlike in the style, with its meticulous precision in summing up the essential. This put the player in the position of trying to guess what was represented, or of wanting to ask: "What is it?" It made one want to know more.

*Le Jeu des petits chevaux* (The Game of Little Horses) put the accent on the four key phases of champagne making: the vineyard and the harvest, the blending, the maturing in the cellar and finally the tasting. Here, too, the game introduced a notion of progression, of time passing.

## Promise of pleasure, symbol of voluptuousness

Red is the new colour adopted by the brand Piper-Heidsieck, notably for the labels of their champagne bottles. The comic book *Moments rouges* (Red Moments) was a sensual exploration of the world of this vibrant colour. It evoked moments in which life takes on a special intensity, which would go well with the enjoyment of Piper-Heidsieck. Jean-Claude Götting's drawings put the accent on the power of red to attract attention, provoke desire and flirt with the taboo. Using strong contrasts with black and white, he dramatised the fatal, passionate aspect of red, as when the action of a film reaches its climax. This treatment established a continuity with the theme of cinema, which Piper-Heidsieck had used as the centrepiece of its promotions for many years.

Christophe MERLIN
**Piper-Heidsieck**
2005 - Birthday portfolio

Why hat are we really watching when we watch television? A channel, a programme or an image? What if we were also watching the television set? Illustration allows us to play with these levels of meaning by inventing visual puns and semantic games. Readers become the viewers of the TV viewers that they are in their own life. The person who is watching becomes the one who is watched. Illustration reinvents tele-reality. Changing the artist brings a change of programme. It is also possible to change the channel. Channels too have an image, technique and motivation that are driven by TV personalities who are strangely familiar to us. They enter our homes through the window of the small screen. And we love to run into them, just as if we had bumped into them in the street.

*Previous page:*

Pierre LE-TAN
**Telefunken**
1995 - Catalogue

## Zapping between lifestyles

What is more present, more familiar or more inevitable in our everyday domestic life than a television? Thomson Multimedia makes and markets televisions and video recorders under three brand names – Saba, Telefunken, Thomson – designed to match the lifestyles of very different types of consumers.

Philippe Starck, who handles the artistic direction of the company's image, asked us to work on a series of projects in which illustration could be used to give prominence to the values of each brand.

Saba is aimed at a target audience that is not particularly keen on technology but more interested in ecology and keeping their equipment down to the bare minimum. We collaborated with Paul Cox on the design of a press kit and packaging that were very "natural" for an experimental television in a chipboard casing, called Jim Nature.

We produced our first catalogue for Telefunken in 1995. For this brand, aimed at "enlightened middle classes", hedonists who know what is good for them, the consumer is simultaneously the source of inspiration and the target audience for scenes designed to have a mirror effect. The presentation of the products designed by Thierry Gauguin, Philippe Starck's right-hand man, reflects an idealised vision of Telefunken's "art of living".

Flicking through the catalogue is like zapping from channel to channel, between different scenes of daily life. On one page, colour images produced by four different illustrators portray the different atmospheres of imagined comfortable interior scenes. Loustal pictures a seaside in the tropics, Floc'h a painter's world, Le-Tan a reassuring family

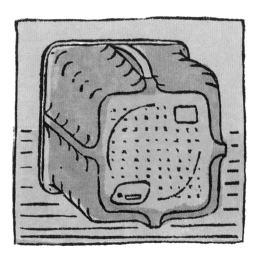

LOUSTAL
**Telefunken**
1995 - Catalogue

BENOIT
**Telefunken**
1995 - Catalogue

house and Benoit a welcoming, flower-filled home. The opposite page features a photo of the corresponding television, switched off. The reader's brain makes the association between the two and imagines the television in the illustrated decor. In reality, the television is not seen in the room scenes, which implies that it is not invasive. In a drawing by Le-Tan, a remote control forgotten on an armchair seems ready to switch on the television that is switched off on the facing page.

For the following year's catalogue, we adopted another strategy: inserting colour images extracted from the previous year's catalogue in the television screens. This created a continuity, an element of fun

Jacques TARDI
**Canal +**
1994 - *Livre anniversaire*

## On automatic Pilote

At the beginning of the 1990s, Canal +, France's first encrypted TV channel, celebrated ten years of existence – ten years dedicated to sport and cinema that made their mark on the French audiovisual landscape through their iconoclasm, inventiveness and radical innovation. The programme that gave the channel its tone was *Nulle Part Ailleurs* (Nowhere Else), directed and presented by Philippe Gildas and Antoine de Caunes, surrounded by a prestigious body of commentators such as Jérôme Bonaldi, Jackie Berroyer, Annie Lemoine, Philippe Vandel and the "Nuls", whose devastating humour gave the programme its original flavour. Several ideas about how to involve subscribers in this anniversary had already flown out

FABRICATION ARTISANALE DU DÉCODEUR.

and a memory stimulus. We kept only one illustrator, Benoit. For the final image he provided the allusion of a dog dozing at night-time, just where Floc'h had depicted a lively cat the previous year.

1. Walter MINUS
2. GOTLIB
3. BINET
Canal +
*1994 - Livre anniversaire*

4. BEN RADIS
5. Martin JARRIE
Canal +
*1994 - Livre anniversaire*

of the creative melting-pot of Canal +. Antoine de Caunes suggested to the head of the birthday operation, Gilles Verlant (a great rock'n'roll expert and biographer of Serge Gainsbourg, among others), that he should entrust us with the task of sorting through all the good ideas and giving form to a definitive project. The time available was very short: nine months. A gestation period in which to gather together creative ideas, capture the spirit of the channel, understand its workings and handle its personalities and hierarchies with diplomacy – as well as eventually conceiving and bringing to fruition a project intended to reproduce the unique style and schoolboy spirit that could be found "nowhere else".

The result was a gift box containing the sounds and images that the channel had produced, decrypted in ten small, completely different books and objects.

*Audio* was a CD that recreated the aural ambiance of the channel: voices, the sounds of the corridors, of offices and studio floors, recorded live. *Chrono*, unfolding like a 13-foot-long accordion, recalled

1. Charlie SCHLINGO
2. François AVRIL
3. LOUSTAL
4. Ever MEULEN
5. Frank MARGERIN
6. WOLINSKI
7. Glen BAXTER
**Canal +**
*1994 - Livre anniversaire*

the key dates and everything that had happened in
the previous ten years. *Scenario* recounted a visit to
Canal + imagined by Jean Teulé, a little envelope-
book stuffed with mythical and iconoclastic objects.
*Mélo* was an elusive photo-novel, written by Albert
Algoud, inset with photos of all the channel's stars.
*Photo* was an album with Xavier Lambours' black and
white snapshots taken in the corridors of the channel.
*Dico* presented an anthology of expressions, words
and formulae specific to certain people on the channel, collected by Gilles Verlant and Marie-Pascale
Lescot. *Crypto* was an amusing explanation of the
process of encrypting and deciphering hidden images and text, prefaced by Jérôme Bonaldi.

In all these booklets, illustrations are scattered
around to serve as a link between the various photographic approaches. In *Portfolio*, however, it took up
the entire space: ten original drawings created specially for the occasion by ten of the greatest illustrators of our age. It was a tribute to comic artists, the
true spiritual fathers of a channel impregnated with
the culture of *Pilote*. According to Pierre Lescure,
who wrote the preface, there are huge numbers of

1

2

... TOUJOURS COMME ÇA, LES SOIRÉES CORRIDA ... SONT JAMAIS D'ACCORD SUR LE RÉSULTAT ...

3

4

5

people at Canal + who grew up on the comic books of the 1960s. In the same spirit, *Studio*, created by Dupuy & Berbérian, was a series of illustrated cut-out sheets that allowed readers to recreate the setting of *Nulle Part Ailleurs* for themselves. The presenters, commentators, technicians and invited guests could be placed in the scenery formed by the end of the book. A special place was reserved for two of the day's guests, with blank faces so that subscribers could insert their own photos.

## Homage to cartoonists
### by Pierre Lescure

My friends call me a collector. No doubt they are referring to my thousands of rock'n'roll singles, Bakelite objects and original plates from my favourite cartoonists. Damn, I've been nabbed! And yet, everything started innocently enough… A childhood lulled to sleep by the heroes created by Vaillant, such as Roudoudou and Riquiqui, Placid and Muzo and Arthur the ghost…Or then again Poïvet's *Pioneers*

6

7

Alain Chabat

Dominique Faruggia

Le public

Chantal Lauby

Le J.T.N.

Bruno Carette

Les standardistes

Cameraman

Philippe Vandel

LES GUIGNOLS L'INFO

NPA

Les guignols de l'info

Jackie

DUPUY & BERBÉRIAN
Canal +
1994 - *Livre anniversaire*

Jérôme Bonaldi

Antoine de Caunes

Vous    Vous

Philippe Gildas

Annie Lemoine

Cameraman

Le bureau

Moniteur

Karl Zéro

La régie

Albert Algoud

Le public

113

of Hope, and *The Avatars of A. Babord* by Eugène Gire… And, in *Spirou*, the cartoons of Franckin, Jijé and Tillieux (ah ! Gil Jourdan and the ineffable Libellule!), then *Pilote* and *Métal Hurlant*: time passed and I refused to grow up, I continued to love all that stuff…

Which all goes to explain my pride in offering you these ten original cartoons, specially created for CANAL+'s tenth birthday by ten of the greatest illustrators of our age. The cartoon by Tardi reminds me of the heroic age of the very first decoders, after we recycled a stock of telephone answering-machine casings… The self portrait of Gotlib, so true to life, reminds me of the jubilation with which I devoured his legendary *Dingodossiers*… This guy initiated us, he made us want to play, to write, to draw – and when I say "us", I am thinking of all the Gotlib fans who prowl the corridors of CANAL +, and there are a lot of them…

Would television ever have had the Histoires, the Nuls, alias the Gilet family, without Binet's *Bidochons*? Without the irresistible abominations of Vuillemin, would Faruggia ever have vomited on "everything that moves" in *La Cité de la Peur*? Are not Wolinski and all the team of *Charlie Hebdo* the spiritual fathers of the *Guignols*?

I'd love to lavish time on all of them, speak about the sensual colours of Loustal, the comedy of Margerin, the rock humour of Dodo and Ben Radis, the surrealism of Glen Baxter… I could dwell on Ever Meulen, my idol, the pioneer of the Clear Line, whose original drawings I collect… Gasp! I've been caught! Caught red handed with acute collectionitis! But anyway, I predict that this precious portfolio will rapidly become a coveted collector's item… Trust me, I'm an expert!

*(Preface to the Portfolio from the* Livre anniversaire*)*

Philippe VUILLEMIN
**Canal +**
1994 - *Livre anniversaire*

Pierre LE-TAN
**Telefunken**
1995 - Catalogue

BENOIT
**Telefunken**
1995 - Catalogue

## TV Series

In the first Telefunken catalogue, while other illustrators created individual images, Floc'h preferred to tell a story as a serial, intercut by other cartoons. It was like flicking channels during a film to see what is on the other side, before taking up the story again. A painter leaves his studio and goes home where his wife is waiting for him… We follow them, one or the other, in the different rooms of their apartment as the evening goes on. In seven images, a story of domestic happiness in a reassuring world reveals the qualities of comfort and tradition in which Telefunken's potential buyers recognise themselves. The television is only suggested, from behind. The reader can imagine it, switched on or switched off. It is present, but does not absorb the life of the characters.

Floc'h often likes to refer to his own personal life. The painter could well be him. The pictures on the walls are works that he has painted himself. And on the small table in front of the woman talking on the telephone, his name figures on the catalogue of a recent exhibition at the Pixi gallery.

Laboratory, from the Latin *laborare*, to work. As in "to elaborate". To experiment, research, prepare… From the idea to the first doodles, then on to the sketch, it is rather like the art of cooking. The chef chooses the ingredients, combines them and then cooks them. He controls the heat of the oven and measures out the seasoning.

During the cooking he lifts the lid of the pot to check the progress. He has a taste and corrects the proportions. When he is satisfied with the effect produced on the taste buds, the eye and the nose, he knows that he's got the recipe right. By adding the final touch, he will be the first to enjoy it.

*- Henri… est-ce possible? une glace au sésame après la salade de homard en gelée de crustacés! Hummm, accord parfait avec votre champagne…Aimez-vous Debussy?*

*- Vous savez docteur, j'ai toujours été fâchée avec les chiffres. Heureusement, Charles Heidsieck m'a réconcilliée avec eux : Mis en Cave en 97, Mis en Cave 96… 95… 94… 93… 92… 91… 90…*

*- Mais vous êtes fous!… pourquoi pas des frites pendant que vous y êtes?*

BENOIT
**Charles Heidsieck**
2001 - Unpublished sketches for the press
kit *Snack Art®* by Charles Heidsieck

Abandoned sketches

Before ending up with the six images
that illustrated this press kit dedicated
to new ways of enjoying champagne,
*Snack Art® by Charles Heidsieck,*
we had to look at many others and
focus on the subject at length before
eventually reaching our destination…
We needed a series of witty images
that would work in counterpoint with
the written content provided by
Daniel Thibault, the Heidsieck
company's talented wine expert, and
the sociologist Jean-Paul Kaufmann.
Benoit was with us throughout our
search, with his innate sense of the
visually absurd.

These four unused sketches confirm
the surreal talent of our friend from
Brussels. When it came to choosing,
some gems of humour unfortunately
had to be discarded. Did we make the
best choice? That's for you to judge.

- Sa période bleue, quelle fraîcheur! Quelle joie!
Il me revient en mémoire ce petit port de Sardaigne, comment s'appelait-il déjà?

121

Anja KROENCKE
**La Grande Épicerie de Paris**
2002 - Sketches for Christmas catalogue

Happy New Year!

As Anja Kroencke lived in New York, we had to communicate by post and fax. We started off by giving her the most precise description possible of the people and situations that had to be portrayed: six Christmas and New Year parties with entirely different characters: a pair of artists, an extremely hip girl about town, an Italian couple in Paris, etc.
We received an initial batch of line drawings, with no details or colouring, which allowed us to assess Anja's interpretation of our characters. After a few comments and corrections, we moved on to the second stage, which involved creating atmosphere by adding colours and secondary characters (party guests). After receiving our go-ahead, Anja set about completing the project with total tranquillity.

Lorenzo MATTOTTI
**Le Printemps**
1997 - Sketches for the store's Christmas card.

Sketches and doodles

Developing an idea involves first turning it around in your mind, producing numerous sketches and letting your pencil explore the possibilities of a line in space in the hope that a suitable approach materialises before your very eyes. This image was intended to illustrate a Christmas card for the Printemps department store: Lorenzo Mattotti managed to find the quintessence of the emotional message with lines that intertwined the female silhouette and the famous dome of the Parisian department store so closely that they become one and the same person, raising her glass of champagne to usher in the New Year.

The creative process

From conception to completion, an
illustrative artwork will pass through
several stages: it is a veritable
obstacle course.
First, the idea must be proposed to the
client, who will then decide whether to
pursue this direction and confirm that
all the brand's strategic elements are
expressed.
A rough sketch is necessary; this
should be precise in its content but
sufficiently open to retain scope for
development. This sketch must of
course be very appealing, but it must
be remembered that this is only an
intermediary stage. Another important
player will soon take the baton: the
chosen illustrator. He or she will take
hold of the idea, make it his or her own
and go beyond it.
In general, the initial sketch is
accompanied by a recommendation for
the choice of illustrator, to clarify the
ideas from the outset.
In the second phase, a skeleton of the
artwork is undertaken by the illustrator
in question, in order to check that all
the concepts have been understood.
At this stage, things can still evolve:
with tact, the smaller details can be
redefined.
This leads us to the final phase, in
which full confidence must be placed
in the illustrator, as the composition,
style, colours and materials are his
or her domain. An illustration is a
collaboration: each person involved
needs the other, and each has
a role to play.

Franck & Fils
1997
1. Sketch by the author
2 and 3. Sketch and final illustration by IZAK

1

2

3

...essoires & Mode 　　Patisseries & Chocolat... 　　Groom

...ssoires et choisir l'Habillé 　　avec Gourmandise et Légèreté

...ssoires et choisir une Robe de Rêve 　　avec Gourmandise et Légèreté

1

2

3

Why hesitate when you know
what you want?

Sometimes one feels compelled to put
artists in competition with each other
in order to get the best out of each of
them, only to end up confirming one's
(admittedly vague) initial instincts.
In this Christmas card for the magazine
*Stratégies*, which specialises in
advertising communication, we had
to express a desire to fight back
against the all-pervading gloom that
characterised this period – 1993.
We chose to depict a character holding
– or wearing on himself – all the
symbols of luck, thereby allowing him
to face the coming new year with a
fistful of trump cards.
The design team was uncertain about
the style to adopt and so wanted to
try out several artists to compare their
approaches.

4

5

muguet

ciel

chiffre 13

trèfle
à 4 feuilles

coccinelle

fer-à-cheval

patte de
lapin

6

Vue sur la ville - 48 04 55 15

7

Le Groupe Stratégies vous souhaite une bonne année 1993?

In such a case, it is preferable to
choose illustrators who have very
different styles. Here, it was Pierre
Le-Tan's project that won the day,
with its graphic vision of the character
bedecked with good-luck charms.
This takes nothing away from the talent
of the other artists in competition on
this occasion.
The value of the operation lay in better
defining the image that the client
wanted to give to his company.

**Groupe Stratégies**
1992 - Carte de vœux 1993
1. Preparatory sketch by the author
2 to 5. Sketches by François AVRIL
6. Sketch by Pierre LE-TAN
7. Pierre LE-TAN's final drawing

2

Emu de se trouver face à l'Univers...

1

**Chanel**
1996 - *Le Conte de Noël*
1. Max CABANES' final illustration
2 and 3. Preparatory sketches by the author

3

Il était une fois un homme seul dans la campagne...

un Soir de Noël ~

Il était parfumeur —

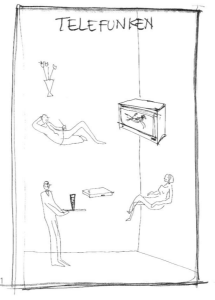

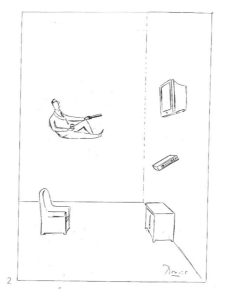

Ping pong

We played ping pong with Benoit by fax for a whole afternoon – the ball being, of course, a drawing. An idea was lobbed over, a detail proposed and it would invariably come back transformed.
Finally, once we moved the TV to a more "overhead" position, everything was set in motion. Elements changed place, expressions varied and the real became surreal.
Benoit draws characters in perfectly normal poses, but he isolates and shifts them into a strange context, a vacuum, and it is that which creates the absurdity.
Why is this character sitting in a void?
And why is that one leaning back, on the point of losing his balance?
And why has that other one got one foot in the air?
It is up to you to find an answer.

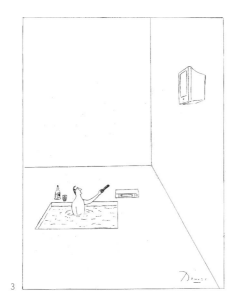

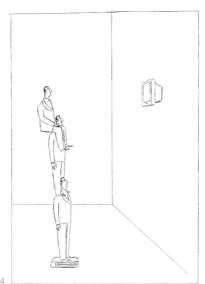

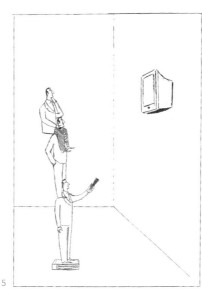

Telefunken
1995
1. Sketch by the author
2 to 8. Sketches by BENOIT
9. Final cover of the catalogue

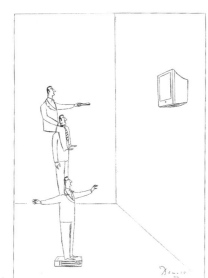

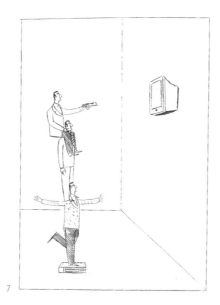

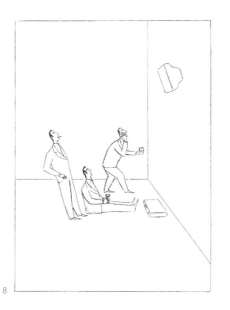

F. 8.9.

— elle n'a pas peur d'être elle même.

"Ça rend les autres jalouses!"

"Des femmes qui ont de l'allure, il y en a sur chaque continent, dans chaque pays ......."

"elle est curieuse de tout!"

"...ça fait un peu peur bien sûr. vous hésitez. Vous vous dites que vous allez être ridicule......"

elle a quelque chose de solaire

IZAK
**Chanel**
*1996 - Sketches for* Le Petit Livre beige
*and the* Allure *playing cards*

"..... c'est exactement vous.
Exactement l'allure....."

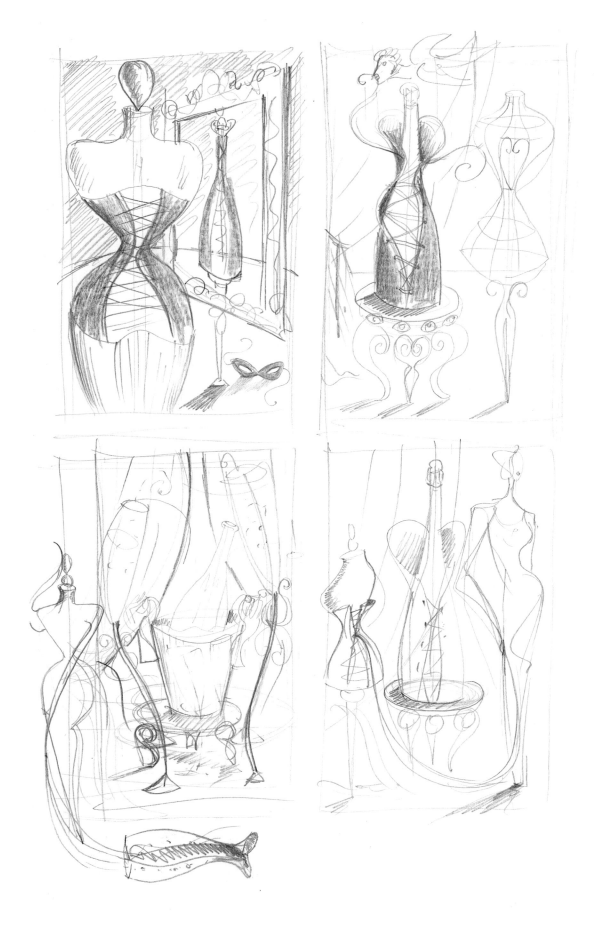

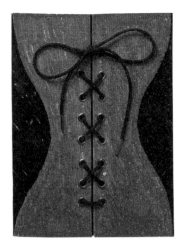

Mïrka LUGOSI
**Piper-Heidsieck**
1998 - Unpublished sketches for a press pack

Undress me!

In 1998, Piper-Heidsieck champagnes launched a special vintage. They asked the couturier Jean Paul Gaultier to "dress" it. His instincts led him towards an extremely sexy vinyl sheath in the brand's colour, a flamboyant red, laced up like a corset.
This series of drawings by Mïrka Lugosi was designed for a publication to be presented to the press – it remained unpublished. Our brief was the following: to give sexy seduction tips, in keeping with the slightly sadomasochistic tone suggested by Jean Paul Gaultier's creation.

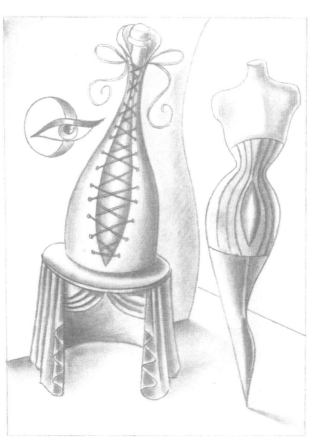

ambiance cosy, lumière spot
contrasté. couleur chaude
allant du sepia très foncé au blanc cassé,
du jaune aussi

TAX de LOUSTAL nom Alain L

telecommande?

LOUSTAL
**Telefunken**
1995 - Sketches and final image
for the catalogue

**Le Savoir-faire**

CAP NORD IMPRESSIONS

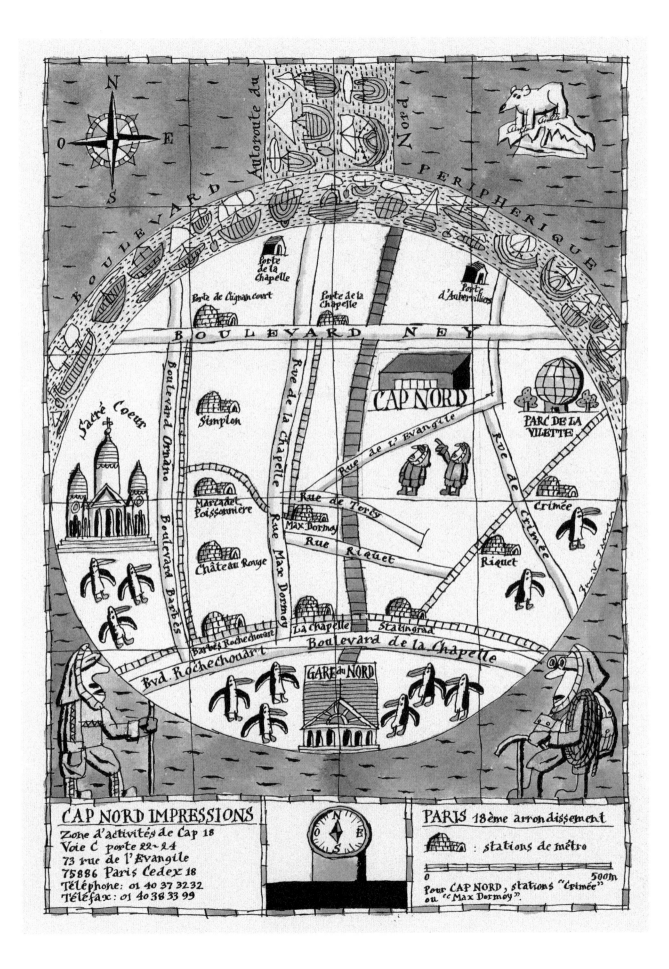

Benoît JACQUES
**Cap Nord Impressions**
1996 - Brochure
Unpublished drawings

An unfinished project

Sometimes everything stops dead, suddenly. A project carried out over the course of many weeks, with client and agency in agreement, can be brought to a halt only a few days before its completion because the advertiser's commercial strategy has moved in another direction. The quality of the work in progress is not in question, but the change is a result of second thoughts or unexpected circumstances in the client's business. These events have to be accepted with fatalism, even though everyone has put all their enthusiasm and passion into organising the project, developing it, combining their talents – copywriting, drawing, designing – and choosing the best supports – paper, textures, formats… Here is a little box of around 15 x 10 cm: it was going to contain a whole range of printed documents on the theme of the North Pole – a reference to the name of our client – in order to explain and present with the aid of specific examples the impressive capacities of this excellent printing house, one of the last to be found in central Paris. The project did not come to fruition; nevertheless, Benoît Jacques had finished the drawings, and the texts had been written. Everything was in place to create, with this little box, a formidable promotional tool aimed at a discerning clientele.

Ever MEULEN
**Chanel**
1992 - Sketches for *Couleurs et Lumière*
Green

Pause for reflection

It is always fascinating to be privy to
an illustrator's approach to a project.
Sketches reveal the beginnings,
choices and changes in direction in the
development of an idea.
It is unfortunately rare to have access
to these preparatory studies. One thing
is certain: as soon as the artist shows
his or her first sketches, the subject is
open for discussion.
An exchange of ideas makes it easier
to settle on the best option. It is also
a way of dispelling an artist's doubts.
This sketch by Ever Meulen allowed
me to enter the construction process
of his drawing and, furthermore,
help him choose the best way out
of the maze!

1

A common platform

Advertising publications sometimes demand the simultaneous creation of both form and content, a search for the right look, size and design matched by a good story to tell.
For the inauguration of the Chanel jewellery boutique in Place Vendôme, we chose to portray the 500 metres advance made by Gabrielle Chanel, over the course of 60 years, from the Faubourg Saint-Honoré to the square. The journey was narrated by the Vendôme column itself, as it was a privileged witness to Chanel's life, day in, day out.
Before presenting our scenario to all concerned – the chief press officers, art director and the Managing Director – I had to sketch the four stages of this route. To evoke Chanel's life in the Ritz Hotel, I drew inspiration from archives of the period – not only photos but also the drawings of the decorator

2

Christian Bérard, a close friend of Chanel. I imagined that a treatment in black and white, set off by just a gold or silver light, depending on the era, would be ideal for recreating the night-time atmosphere.

To get projects moving, it is often essential to pass through this stage of sketches or scribbles, in order to explain, convince or charm, but also to come to grips with the ideas that are starting to form. These sketches also make it possible to give a precise briefing at the next stage and to guide the illustrator along the path I have laid out.

When we outlined the sketch of an illustration intended for a publicity brochure for Veuve Clicquot champagne, the idea was to show, in the same image, several great writers who had lived at very different times, all raising a toast in honour of the company's founder.

An annotated sketch guides an illustrator, allowing him or her free rein as regards composition, style and displays of technique. This scene, which brings together Sacha Guitry, Gogol, Pushkin and Proust, is made wonderfully credible by the talent of Floc'h.

**Chanel Joaillerie**
1997 - *Chez Mademoiselle,*
*18, place Vendome*
1. François AVRIL's final illustration
2. Sketch by the author

**Veuve Clicquot**
1995 - Brochure *À la recherche*
*de la perfection*
3. Sketch by the author

4

Jeunesse

beauté        mode        Richesse

5

6

Walter MINUS
Chanel
1996 - *Le Conte du Temps Présent*
1 to 6. Preparatory sketches by the author

Pour cet été la véritable
Je propose
Sauterelle du Togo au Gandujaaaaa

Secret
Safari
Punk

Une autre
Cacao
Carotte
Pour
le rayon
Velouté !

Walter MINUS
Dog Generation
2001 - Sketch for the press pack of
*Oh My Cat!*

Evolution and transformation

From Elizabeth I to Claudia Schiffer
was a big leap, but our client was
adamant: "Away with the ruff around
her neck and the uptight hairdo, let her
hair down and show off her shoulders".
This was how a quite elaborate
preparatory drawing paved the way for
a last-minute development that was
definitely on the right track, leading
towards a reference with a greater
power of suggestion than we had ever
imagined at the outset.

Éric GIRIAT
La Grande Épicerie de Paris
2006 - Sketches for the brochure *Backstage*

The benefit of choice

Quite frequently a subject can be
so rich that the illustrator hesitates
between several ideas and so
proposes various ways of tackling it.
Along with both the illustrator and the
client, we extricate the essentials.
Afterwards, the illustrator can put a
final polish on the solution we have
adopted.

Marion → Laurent.

Je sais que c'est beaucoup de bou-lot. Tu fais juste une esquisse. Juste pour qu'ils aient un idée.

Bon, là c'est pas dans les proportions. Mais l'idée

C'est de les voir plus de dos. Toujours l'un derrière l'autre.
Elle, un peu genre Sophia Loren en équilibre sur les étoiles.....

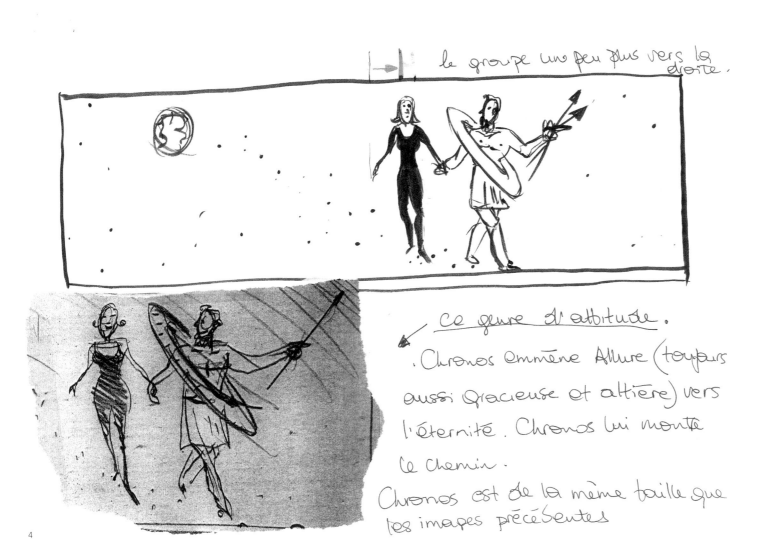

le groupe une peu plus vers la droite.

Ce genre d'attitude.

· Chronos emmène Allure (toujours aussi gracieuse et altière) vers l'éternité. Chronos lui monte le chemin.

Chronos est de la même taille que les images précédentes

4

5

A final image is never definitive

Sometimes a detail takes on great importance and we are obliged to reconsider what we have taken for granted. Here is one example: in the final frame of a Charlie Chaplin film, or in the last square of the adventures of Lucky Luke, the hero strides towards his destiny. The creator expresses this by showing the character from the back, facing his future. I had the feeling that this was the example to follow to complete this *Conte du Temps Présent* illustrated by Walter Minus. Our discussions with the client showed us that it was better to view things from the opposite angle, in order to make it more positive. Therefore, Cronos and the goddess Allure advance towards a radiant future by walking towards us, the reader. Perhaps – who knows? – to take us with them.

6

**Chanel**
1996 - *Le Conte du Temps Présent*
1, 4 and 5. Sketches by the author
2 and 3. Sketches by Walter MINUS
6. Walter MINUS' final illustration

Jewellery instils a desire for irrational splendour. The image thus becomes the jewellery box. It gives beauty its meaning and translates the value of the jewel into promises of emotion. Simplicity is often the best solution, however, and a hint can say more than an emphatic declaration. Night reveals the light, the brilliance of a diamond, the hidden magic of precious stones, the secret thrill of pearls; it provides a velvety setting for a dream of luxury and sensual delight. Humour, on the other hand, can serve modernity, underline creative daring and introduce a casual youthfulness into a new relationship between women and jewellery.

## An unusual bestiary

Taking inspiration from the Fables of La Fontaine to present a collection of jewellery in verse was a daring project that Chanel was quick to accept. The bestiary, a line of jewels in the form of animal charms, is a prerequisite for jewellers as international demand is always high. For Chanel, this traditional line had a rather conventional side that needed to

### The Elephant and the Tortoise

*A lumbering Elephant lamented his fate*
*To a Tortoise who gleamed in a bright carapace.*
*The sharp-spoken reptile couldn't help but berate*
*His ponderous pal's utter absence of grace.*

*"They mocked me as slow when colour I lacked,*
*But now they all envy my lustrous curves!*
*Dress up! Splash out! Go smarten your act!*
*Win all the renown that an Elephant deserves! "*

*Now spangled with sapphire, bedecked with fine pearls,*
*Diamonds and gold – a real spending spree!*
*His bulk now majestic, to thunderous applause,*
*He looks royal, he is splendid, with a bound he is free!*

*"Money is the key to freedom",*
*And diamonds are a girl's best friend;*
*Extravagance rules in beauty's kingdom –*
*for the world's more beautiful when you spend!*

*Previous page:*

François AVRIL
**Chanel Joaillerie**
*1997 - Chez Mademoiselle, 18, place Vendôme*

be "ruffled up" before the collection was presented to the press.

Before Françoise Aveline proposed writing *Les Fables impertinentes* (The Fanciful Fables), she had matched up the animals in a way that suited the stories she had in mind. After we had seen the jewels, however, we had to reconsider the project in visual terms so that the sizes of the animals corresponded to each other in the composition and the image. She had to reinvent the stories of the Stag and the Hedgehog, the Elephant and the Tortoise, the Lion, the Cock and the Frogs, the Fish, and then find quotations from Coco Chanel which worked as morals for the stories. Artistic directors can be tyrants at times!

We have definitively broken the codes of jewellery advertising by juxtaposing these texts with the illustrations of Clare Mackie. Her style – caricatured, poetic and good-natured but also figurative – estab- lishes a degree of detachment, demonstrating that the sumptuousness of jewellery does not preclude a capacity to laugh at oneself. Just as Chanel had always wished, jewels are still primarily a source of amusement.

Clare MACKIE
**Chanel Joaillerie**
1998 - *Les Fables impertinentes de Chanel*

Clare MACKIE
**Chanel Joaillerie**
1998 - *Les Fables impertinentes de Chanel*

### The Stag and the Hedgehog

*A prickly Hedgehog, weary of spines,*
*Decided one day he would capture the moon.*
*He told the proud Stag of his lunar designs,*
*But the Stag dreamed only of reaching the sun.*

*They vowed to accomplish this wildest of plans,*
*With naught but unwavering faith in their hearts,*
*Yet the Stag sprang aloft with such graceful élan,*
*That his antlers snagged several sharp golden darts.*

*The Hedgehog bided his time in the gloom,*
*Then pricking the face of the star with his bristles*
*He stole a few silvery moondrops which soon*
*Glistened like genuine pearls in his prickles.*

*"Play on your failings, make the most of your faults",*
*As Mademoiselle would so often tell us,*
*She would have smiled on these creatures' revolt*
*For they'd used their shortcomings to conquer the heavens.*

**The Lion, the Rooster and the Frogs**

*Two young Frogs seeking lessons in elegance*
*Found in the Lion and the Rooster fine teachers.*
*Their counsel, astute and full of intelligence,*
*Is, truth to tell, good for all living creatures.*

*"Stay master of colour and style," said the bird,*
*His plumage brilliant with rainbow flashes,*
*"If you know yourself well and dare to be heard,*
*You will surely make the most of your assets."*

*"To each his own style," the mighty Lion agreed,*
*As he tossed his mane rippling with light,*
*"I love to dazzle, so fire is my creed,*
*Jewels suit me best when they are bright."*

*"The way to success so often lies*
*Off the beaten path of learning."*
*So let your instinct be your guide -*
*You will find it more than discerning.*

**The Fish who wanted to see the World**

*A trio of slender, daring Fish*
*Dreaming on the ocean floor*
*Solemnly made a heroic wish*
*To see the world as never before.*

*Knowing the perils lurking there*
*They stole the water's brilliant sheen*
*And dressed their precious scales with care*
*In subtle shades of blue and green.*

*Beauty made them bright and bold*
*The oceans' treasures were theirs to keep.*
*They gleamed with amethyst and gold,*
*As the sun sank violet into sleep.*

*The moral of the tale's a pearl*
*From Mademoiselle, who always said:*
*"The world's an oyster for the girl*
*Who has the wit to see ahead."*

*Françoise Aveline*

155

## A sophisticated scrap book

Illustrations can provide a breath of fresh air that immediately establishes an intimacy between the artist and the reader. This factor led us to ask Pierre Le-Tan to present a jewellery collection inspired by the sea. We plumped for a quirky reworking of the normally "polished" image of Chanel's publicity material to create a surprising effect that moved in the opposite direction from luxury and heightened emotion.

Structurally, the work revolved around the three seaside towns that marked the life of Gabrielle Chanel: Deauville, Biarritz and Roquebrune. And we imagined the little book of notes and sketches that she had with her when she was on the beach.

Pierre Le-Tan reproduced the atmosphere of real photos of the time. In the style of a scrap book, he positioned little fragments of inspiration around the image: shells, starfish, waves, which are reflected in the form and spirit of the jewels in the collection. The effect is very touching, as it really conveys the impression of looking at a personal photo album. This sets up an intimacy, a proximity that is also implicit in the title, *Gabrielle à la plage* (Gabrielle at the Seaside), written by hand. It communicates naturalness and simplicity, which complement the luxury of the jewels and the refinement of the album. We brought out a numbered edition of 999 copies bound by a cord inspired by sail sheets.

*gabrielle à la plage*

Pierre LE-TAN
**Chanel Joaillerie**
*1996 - Gabrielle à la plage*

Tourbillons, torsades, j'aime
les formes qui s'enroulent

Le 28 Juin 1913. Deauville

Trésors trouvés
hier dans mes poches

Le coquillage est un
labyrinthe. J'irai plusieurs
vies. Sait-on d'où il
vient ? où il va ?

Boy Capel

La plage

Je reviens toujours aux formes de la nature

La Vénus de Botticelli

20 Juillet 1916
Biarritz

Décidément, la sphère est la perfection même...

D'où me vient cette passion pour les perles?

158

Le qui compte, c'est le mouvement

Roquebrune, Août 1928

L'eau, une force qui me régénère

La vague, un rythme incessant

Pierre LE-TAN
**Chanel Joaillerie**
*1996 - Gabrielle à la plage*

## Jewels in the night sky

This catalogue is a homage to Paul Iribe, who was Gabrielle Chanel's artistic director in the early 1930s. He was an advertising pioneer, who created, among others, the beautiful publicity brochures with reprographed drawings for Nicolas wines. The night was one of his favourite subjects.

We imagined this theme handled in his style. The background to the images is dark, very detailed, with elements in the near and middle distance portrayed in silhouettes like shadow puppets. The stars and comets – emblems of Chanel's jewellery – the city lights, the reflections on the water and the pieces of jewellery appear like precious stones set in the image. By alternating different kinds of paper one could present the jewellery on a beautiful art paper, in contrast to the illustrations and the text, which were printed on a soft matt paper. Everything accentuated the feeling of depth. Night appears here like a three-dimensional jewel box.

François AVRIL
**Chanel Joaillerie**
*1997 - Chez Mademoiselle,
18, place Vendôme*

## In the footsteps of Mademoiselle

The work of an art director in preparation for the creation of images is sometimes so comprehensive that the illustrator is left with very little room for personal expression. Nevertheless, François Avril has been able to find his creative freedom in this context, when we had to produce a press pack for the opening of the new Chanel Joaillerie boutique in one of the most beautiful mansion houses on Place Vendôme.

François Avril, a longtime collaborator, was an obvious choice, as he was capable of understanding and adapting himself to constraints of style and references that could not be ignored. A great deal was at stake: the fashion house, for so long synonymous with the rue Cambon, had to prove the legitimacy of its status as a jeweller and its eligibility among the most prestigious jewellery names in the world. The establishment of the company at 18, place Vendôme was presented as the logical outcome of Gabrielle Chanel's personal, creative and geographical path. We noticed Chanel had moved some 500 metres in 60 years, in a straight line running from the rue du Faubourg-Saint-Honoré to rue Cambon, then to the Ritz and finally to place Vendôme. Thus, the Vendôme column became the pivot of our scenario, pictured like a character who, every night, watched over Chanel, a tiny light shining in the city. The viewer approaches her through lit windows.

François AVRIL
**Chanel Joaillerie**
1997 - *Chez Mademoiselle,
18, place Vendôme*

164

The story started on a night in 1932, when Chanel launched her first jewellery collection, entirely composed of diamond pieces, in her mansion house in the Faubourg Saint-Honoré. This event and the style of the jewellery presented are the original references that underpin today's output. Later, Chanel's apartment on rue Cambon was linked to her work with precious stones, and her suite at the Ritz to her taste for pearls. Number 18, place Vendôme represented the synthesis of all these sources of inspiration.

Illustration allowed us to create a logic of continuity. We chose to give it a 1930s look, a nod to Chanel's artistic direction during that period, reworked to give it a timeless modernity. François Avril is passionate about Art Deco. After consulting the archives and photos of the era, we tried out different treatments for the images to capture a soft focus that encompassed both past and present. Making the most of the unity of place – the 1st arrondissement – the writer came up with the idea of letting the Vendôme column itself tell the story of Mademoiselle's career. To check

the feasibility of this viewpoint, and see what the area looked like from above, we obtained special permission to climb to the top of the column via the interior staircase. All the tourists wanted to follow us inside! We worked on the content of the images from an exterior point of view, as if they were seen through the windows of each of the places evoked: this provided a narrative dimension that added intensity. The cinematic side of the composition was emphasised by the treatment in black and white – Chanel's colours – set off by the application of alternate small areas of gold and silver. Each image appeared like a jewel box that set off the light of a chandelier or a jewel.

François AVRIL
**Chanel Joaillerie**
*1997 - Chez Mademoiselle,*
*18, place Vendôme*

Tinou LE JOLY SENOVILLE
**Boucheron**
*1998 - Le Joaillier-Parfumeur*

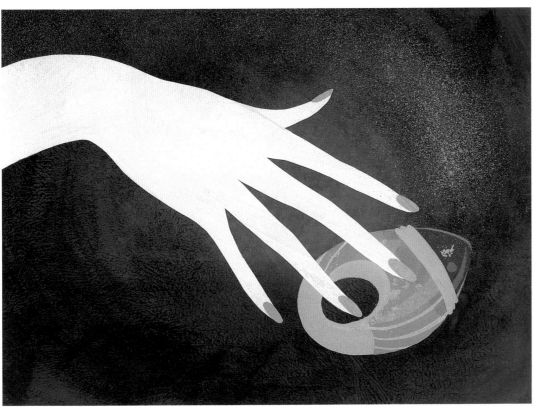

## Art and matter

For a jeweller, like a perfumer, the essence is the art of working with nature's riches: stones, flowers or fruit – raw materials metamorphosed by talent. By building bridges between the two crafts, Boucheron made an image for its brand.

In the generic press pack, the visuals mixed and married two languages of seduction. Tinou Le Joly Senoville is an illustrator of "matter". She basically works with collages, cut-up paper and splashes of paint, combining and superimposing elements. This manual approach seemed very appropriate for the skills we wanted to evoke, with their emphasis on volume, composition and craftsmanship.

The ever-present blue background recalled the company's emblematic colour. By mixing flat colours and transparency, the illustrator established a depth that reflected the feeling of opening a jewellery box, or staring into a sapphire, Boucheron's trademark stone. There is a magic, a sensory emotion that is almost tactile. The showers of gold evoke the toned gold that is one of the most recognisable features of the Boucheron style. They also recreated the enveloping feeling of perfume as "olfactory jewellery", like a precious but invisible diamond necklace. The images played with the meeting of the two worlds, the parallel inspirations and the overlapping of genres in combinations such as perfume-ring and perfume-jewel. There is something theatrical and extremely elegant about the style. The lightness and poetry of line breathed life and youthfulness into the brand, making it look very relevant today.

**M**achines, offices, factories, products, computers, systems, figures… Is it possible to have efficiency and performance without creativity and imagination? With a few pencil marks, illustration brings another, often forgotten, dimension to life. Business professionals find themselves surprised, like the characters of a gripping adventure. Their everyday life fades into the background. Robots become human. With a skilful hand, with humour, talent and complicity, the artist puts colour into rules, ruffles up objectives, reinvents perspectives. In a single line, he adds an element of dreams to the world of business and makes life that bit more exciting.

*Previous page:*

Jean-François MARTIN
**Masaï**
2003 - Brochure

LOUSTAL
**ECS**
1988 - Annual report

## When drawing creates an image

At first sight, what can be drier than a company's annual report? Unless it becomes a pretext for communication aims that extend further than a mere list of results. This was the option taken by Gilles Tugendhat, the chairman of ECS (European Computer System), a firm that, in the mid-1980s, started hiring out high-power computer equipment and the services that go with it to major companies. With the help and friendship of Claude Dimont-Mellac, the Public Relations Director of ECS, we would, over the course of the years, use the annual report to construct a brand image for ECS, employing illustration to invoke in visual terms the counterpoint of technological one-upmanship.

The first year the emphasis was on the way in which ECS was heading for world domination by means of its overseas subsidiaries. Loustal portrayed the capitals of the countries where ECS was established: France, the USA, Japan, the United Kingdom, Germany, Belgium, Italy and Switzerland. The chairman and other senior management figures are also portrayed by the artist. The company comes over as a large domain ripe for adventure.

We then collaborated for three successive years with Philippe Weisbecker. This Frenchman who had lived for many years in the United States was used to illustrating subjects linked to the world of industry and finance. He brought poetry and a picturesque quality through his meticulously constructed drawings, alive with rhythm, volume and geometric figures. His work largely contributed to giving ECS a modern and dynamic image, not only with the financiers but also with its clients and prospective customers.

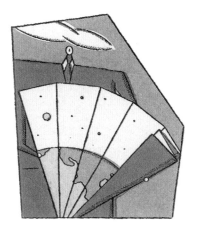

Philippe WEISBECKER
**ECS**
1992 - Annual report

## The master of figures and letters

Pierre Clément is known for his little "robotic" figures. He was particularly conspicuous in the 1980s, thanks to his collaborations with Renault and Reynolds pens. To illustrate the cover of the commercial brochure for Proland, a subsidiary of ECS that develops software packages, he created the character of a circus performer who tames numbers and letters. The moving cylinder on which he is balancing conveys the company's flexibility and adaptability. The rapid scrolling of perspectives evokes the performance of the software packages. The illustration plays on two dimensions: behind a window, the figures and letters seem to float anarchically in a space that looks a bit like a swimming pool; in the foreground, dominated by the tamer, everything is in order. Clément's style abounds in energy, dynamism and rapidity, and the results are highly effective.

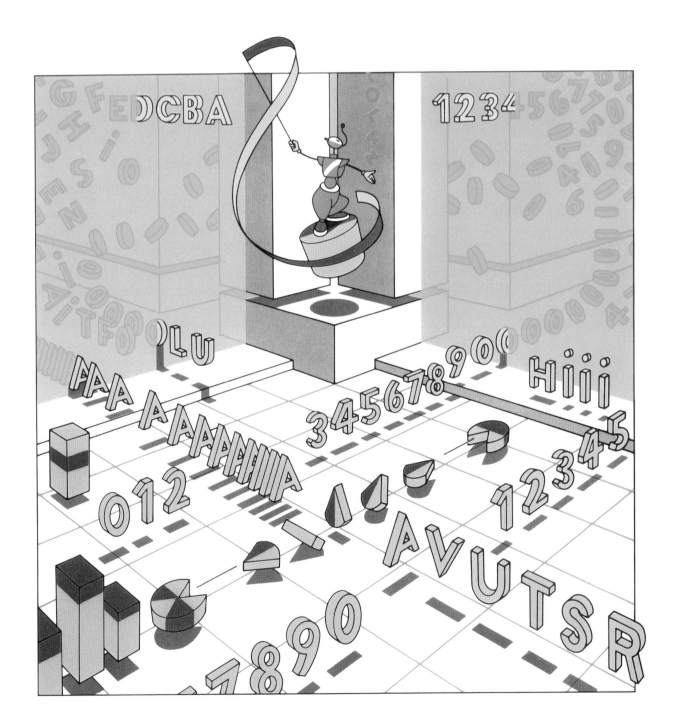

Serge CLERC
**ECS**
1990 - Invitation card and programme

## In perfect harmony

Every year ECS involves itself in the corporate sponsorship of music events. These give the company a chance to conceive visual settings which not only explore different graphic approaches but also contribute to the construction of an authentic brand image. In 1990 Serge Clerc recreated the graphic style of the 1930s for the invitation and programme for a concert in the Salle Pleyel, drawing inspiration from the Art-Deco facade of the concert hall. He is probably one of the greatest colourists of our "gang": the lightness of watercolour allowed him to play with the finest subtleties of his palette. The result was distinguished by its great delicacy and refinement.

## An invitation to the Château

The atmosphere created by Tardi for an invitation to a concert in the chapel of the Château of Versailles is something else altogether – nocturnal, mysterious, impregnated with the site's historical power. The recipients must have had the feeling of being invited to a select event, redolent of prestige and nobility. They could almost believe Louis XIV himself would welcome them into the courtyard, mounted on his horse? Altogether different is this orchestra drawn in black and white, recalling a stave. The viewer seems to be sucked into an image of musical notation. It is at once intense, energetic and highly evocative.

Jacques TARDI
**ECS**
1990 - Invitation card and programme

Frédéric BORTOLOTTI
**ECS**
1989 - Invitation card

Philippe WEISBECKER
ECS
1992 - Invitation for a trip to Tunisia

## An invitation to travel

Personalising an invitation to go on a trip gives meaning to the initiative of the person who has organised it. To present a trip to Tunisia offered by ECS, we pictured an amusing folded invitation, a little work of art to keep. Philippe Weisbecker produced a colourful and attractive screen print, with a few clues scattered around a camel to evoke the country. Philippe knew Tunisia very well as he had lived there for several years. This familiarity is conveyed by the unerring choice of colours, which would not have been so suited to a country like Morocco.

A year later, on the same principle, Benoît Jacques illustrated an invitation for a trip to Quebec organised for the ECS sales team. The care put into the production of the invitation made the recipient feel valued. In this case, it reflected the fact that their work was appreciated by the company. Humour and allusion engender a feeling of happiness and presage happy times of adventure and relaxation.

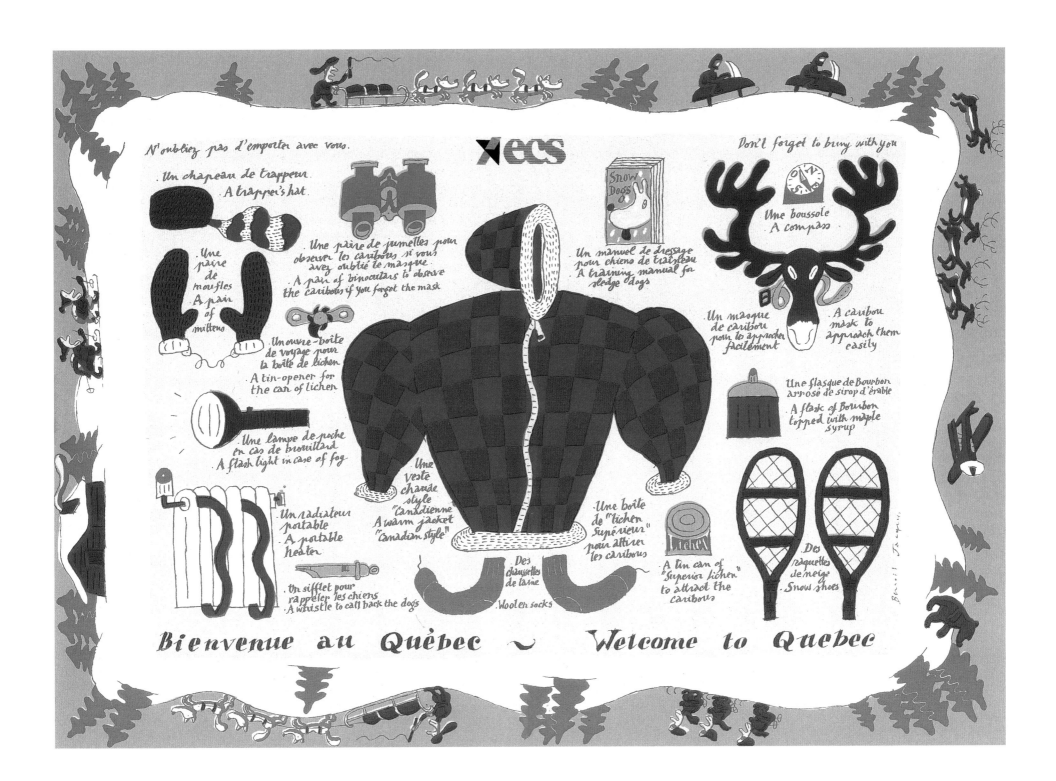

Benoît JACQUES
ECS
1993 - Invitation for a trip to Quebec

Jean-François MARTIN
**Masaï**
2002 to 2004 - Brochures

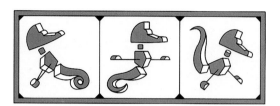

## Company culture

Supporting artistic creation is the vocation of a corporate sponsor, which assures its own renown by associating its name with prestigious events. Sponsorship can also correspond to a real taste for the arts on the part of its directors, thereby endowing their company with genuine cultural status.

This was the case with Silicom, a company that gives guidance to engineers about information technology. Since its creation, its directors, Christian Bataille and Martine Guinot, who are passionate about comic books, have sought to adorn their workplace with the images they love. Almost two hundred screen prints and lithographs by cartoonists already decorated the walls of the head office when we suggested that they should attend an opening in the Christian Desbois gallery, where Loustal was exhibiting nineteen pastels. The result was love at first sight. Christian Bataille fell quite dramatically under the charm of these creations, which marked a radical turn in the artist's work. He asked us to introduce him to the gallery owner, to whom he announced his intention to buy… the entire exhibition. Christian Desbois passed on the proposal to Loustal, who accepted, although he was slightly apprehensive that his work would never be seen by the public once it became the property of Silicom. The following solution was therefore agreed: after a private presentation to Silicom's partners and clients in the company's building, the Loustal collection would be exhibited in the Angoulême Museum of Fine Art, as part of the 18th International Comic Book Festival. We produced the catalogue, prefaced by François Landon and printed in 380 copies, each numbered and signed by the artist. It was a unique occasion for enthusiasts to discover or revisit these works, which form part of a corpus that is now highly prized by collectors.

A little earlier, we had designed the logo for Silicom. Pierre Clément invented for the occasion an original animal in a graphic style that recalled a stylised sea horse. It was portrayed in three postures, three images juxtaposed to express the touchstones of Silicom, which embody the approach that enables them to offer top-quality services: to listen, think and act. It has now become the company's favourite animal and mascot – two years later we used it to illustrate the company's calendar. Christian Bataille and Martine Guinot thoroughly enjoy meeting the artists: we had the opportunity to introduce them to Floc'h. He had been commissioned to do a screen print to announce the creation of Silinet, a subsidiary of Silicom. This was magnificently produced by Éric Seydoux's print shop in Paris. Its idea of letters falling on a fleeing man would not have seen the light were it not for the humour of Christian Bataille and his innate capacity to understand the impact of an image imbued with tongue-in-cheek comedy.

Pierre CLÉMENT
**Silicom**
1990 - Logo

LOUSTAL
**Silicom**
1990 - Exhibition catalogue

FLOC'H
**Silicom**
1988 - Screen print

# UN ENNUI N'ARRIVE JAMAI SS EUL

Après Silicom, Silinet.

Pierre CLÉMENT
**Silicom**
1992 - Brochure

## Welcome to space-time

Mastering the world of computers means penetrating space-time. Silicom's vocation is to help clients in this conquest. This is a rather abstract concept for the uninitiated, but a very significant one for the recipients of the company's presentation brochure. Pierre Clément, who is an architect by training and an expert in the art of representing volumes, produced this superb illustration. The transparency and lightness of the treatment make the changes in perspective and spatial relationships effortless, predictable and comprehensible. His graphic work combines geometry with fluidity, served by translucent colours that are both ethereal and intense. His approach is informed by a strong imagination. The emblematic sea horse is the pretext for an animal phantasmagoria which symbolises the mastery, power and competitiveness acquired by Silicom's clients in the jungle of the business world.

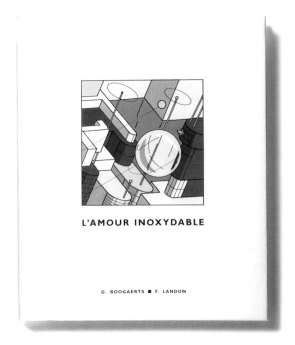

Gilles BOOGAERTS
**Trois Vallées**
1990 - *L'Amour inoxydable*
Text : François Landon

## Breaking eggs in science fiction

The high-end technology developed on certain industrial sites is sometimes so far ahead of its time that it resembles science fiction.

This was the case with the high-tech factory in Mayenne, where the company Trois Vallées separates the yolk and white of eggs to make products for the food industry. When Trois Vallées took part in SIAL, the International Food Salon, in 1990, the company directors, Jean-Michel and Christian Corson, were looking for an original means of getting across the revolutionary procedures used in their factory. Their intention was to produce a document which would benefit their brand image rather than explain in detail an extremely sophisticated technological process. As they were looking above all for an "idea", Martine Barnabé, the project director, asked us to meet them.

The visit to the factory, which is entirely automated, revealed a world we could never even have imagined. "Breaking eggs is easy, the machine does that for us, but what makes our work interesting is conserving the egg's bacteriological and physico-chemical qualities," write Jean-Michel and Christian Corson in the preface of the small book we produced for them, under the inspiration of both science fiction and picture books.

*L'Amour inoxydable* (Stainless-steel love) is the title of a novel written by François Landon. It humanises the subject by telling a love story involving an egg's yolk and white, thereby tracing the path through the different treatments applied to them in the labyrinthine technological process. To emphasise the concept of the "high-tech lab", we designed a cover in screen-printed Perspex for part of the print run, while the other copies had a cardboard cover.

We asked Gilles Boogaerts, an expert in applied geometry, to do the illustrations. With an economy of materials and colours, he succeeded in conveying the factory's modernity and clinical purity. His "sterile" drawing technique was well-suited to the notion of traceability. His futuristic vision of the production line resembled an aerial view of a town seen from an interplanetary capsule. He used axometric perspectives, in which all the lines are parallel. His clean, pure lines and use of strong colours recall the Bauhaus. It must be remembered as well that these drawings were produced before the advent of DTP, and therefore executed entirely by hand, with a set-square, ruler and compass.

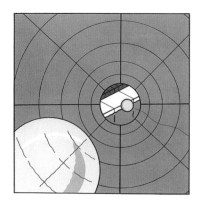

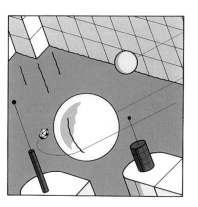

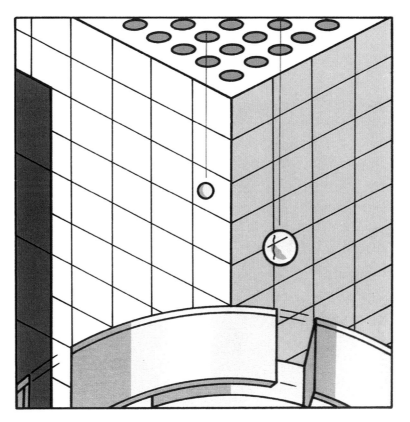
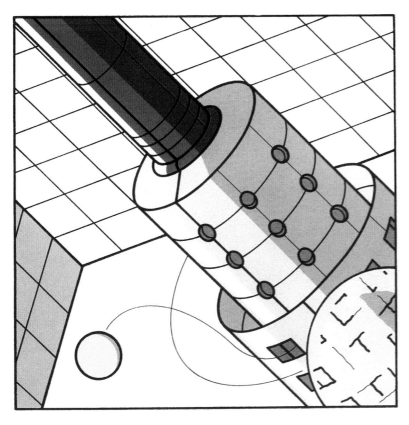
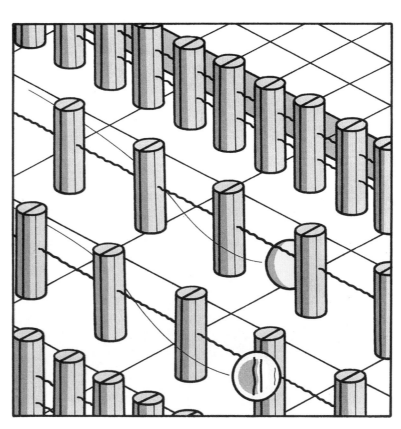

"Le mot topologie est plus souvent à prendre dans son sens "logique" et non pas "géographique". "

Le gestionnaire de réseau désigne entre autre le responsable supervisant le fonctionnement d'un réseau.

L'architecture est le cadre général fixant les règles de communication entre les divers éléments d'un réseau.

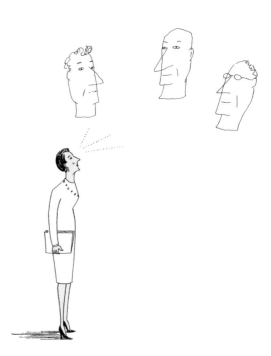

Le signal est une représentation physique, généralement électrique, d'une information en cours de transmission.

BENOIT
**EDF**
1993 - *Le Dicommunicant*

## In the jargon of the trade…

Each professional field has its own vocabulary. In order to fulfil its mission of transporting and distributing electrical energy, EDF uses various telecommunication procedures. This is a world that employs a terminology that is virtually incomprehensible to the layman. To make it accessible and encourage the correct usage of these terms by EDF employees who are confronted with them,

a small practical guide was devised: *Le Dicommunicant* is a pocket glossary, easy to keep in the office and to refer to whenever necessary. The choice of paper and type – the result of much hard work – make it a small object that is pleasant to use. Benoit's cartoons, highlighted by captions taking the terms in the dictionary word by word, give it a surreal dimension that puts a slight distance between the reader and the subject, while avoiding dryness through the use of humour.

L'ÉMULATION EST SURTOUT UTILISÉE POUR QU'UN
TERMINAL D'UNE MARQUE DONNÉE PUISSE DIALOGUER AVEC
UN ORDINATEUR D'UNE AUTRE MARQUE.

LE DÉSASSEMBLAGE EST UNE OPÉRATION CONSTITUANT À
REMETTRE SOUS LEUR FORME "ORIGINALE" LES INFORMATIONS
REÇUES À TRAVERS UN RÉSEAU À COMMUTATION DE PAQUETS.

" SAVIEZ-VOUS QUE LE NUMÉRIQUE EST UN MODE DE
TRANSMISSION EN LANGAGE BINAIRE, C'EST-À-DIRE
EN UNE SUITE D'ÉTATS LOGIQUE "0" ET "1"

" JE LIS ICI QUE DANS LE MODÈLE OSI LA FONCTION
DE ROUTAGE EST ASSURÉE DANS LA COUCHE 3 ! "

- LE VISIOPHONE. -

## All in it together

From the very beginning of Vue sur la Ville, we have wanted to involve our favourite illustrators in the production of something special for the Christmas season. The first year, we sent a long strip of paper, one metre long by thirty centimetres wide all over Paris. Over a fortnight, it circulated, rolled up in its cardboard tube, from artist to artist, each one adding his own image to the one that went before. Fourteen illustrators participated in the creation of a real panoramic fresco: our first greetings card!

These "views of the city" by our collaborators, endowed with their wit, talent and different forms of expression, inspired us to produce the now traditional calendar in which, since 1991, we have invited illustrators to represent a month of the year. Some of them are well known, others less so.

For us, it is always a pleasure mixing surprise and wonder to concoct a work that we know people will look forward to and keep.

Frédéric BORTOLOTTI
Isabelle DERVAUX
Yves CHALAND
François AVRIL
Régis FRANC
Walter MINUS
Jean-Philippe DELHOMME
FLOC'H
Pierre CLÉMENT
Jean-Claude GÖTTING
Jacques TARDI
Serge CLERC
**Vue sur la Ville**
1989 - Agency greetings card

Pour **1990**

qui a vu quelle ville?

**T**he invention of the wheel gave rise to the invitation to travel, to move from place to place — but in what, and where? Our means of transport open up the world to us. In simple, clean lines or elaborate drawings, illustration can sum up a world or lifestyle at a glance. It reinvents in its own way the relationship between the car and the city or its environment. The art of road travel can become art, full stop. And comic books transform the discovery of a region into a thrilling adventure. Promises of sensations, of changes of scene, of the good life, here or elsewhere…

"Draw me a car!" demands the 21st-century Little Prince.

*Previous page:*

LOUSTAL
**Telefunken**
1995 - Catalogue

CARLOTTA
**Renault**
2001 - *L'Atelier Renault*

## When car meets culture

Architect, scenographer, museographer, Franck Hammoutene is famous for his projects in the culture domain: Cité de la Musique, Palais de Tokyo, Théâtre des Champs-Élysées. Yet he was Renault's choice for the revamp of the famous Pub Renault on the Champs-Élysées, a meeting point and symbolic address for a whole generation.

With a new design and a new positioning, it became the Atelier Renault. It serves as both a showcase and an expression of the brand's modernity. This flexible, modular space on the cutting edge is designed to hold exhibitions and a variety of other events. It opened – symbolically – in the year 2000, projecting Renault into the 21st century and the new millennium. The opening coincided with the launch of the Avantime, a model with a completely unexpected design. The press pack produced for this occasion expressed the Atelier Renault's desire to be a place of change and movement. It was made up of individual index cards that can be removed and shuffled. The illustration emphasised the company's creative, conceptual and artistic ambitions while making space for its practical aspects. So, Benoit pictured

François AVRIL
**Renault**
*2000 - L'Atelier Renault*

the Avantime fixed to the wall like a contemporary sculpture. The position of the characters in the pictorial space broke with the brand's traditional image and invited the viewer to take a new look at the car. François Avril recreated the Atelier in the style of an architect's drawing, integrating it into a superb transparent panorama of the Champs-Élysées while making it seem accessible to the public. The vehicles streaming along the front of the image suggest a place that is open to a world that attaches enormous importance to the car.

## On the road, European style

When Renault launched the R19, Europe was an idea that had come a long way. Free circulation was a concept that married well with this mid-range estate car. The abolition of frontiers meant that Renault could escape from its image as a specifically French brand to assert a more international standing.

For the presentation brochure, photos were taken in five different countries: France, Spain, Germany, England and Italy. We played around with the transposition of sensations; by setting a cosy scene in an English manor, for example, we suggested the comfort of the car. Illustration allowed us to create flexibility between technological information and location photographs.

The illustrations punctuated the brochure, evoking the countries presented in the same way as tourist snapshots or holiday memories. They humanised the discourse, and feminised it too – which is important, as women have a big say in the choice of a family car. Le-Tan's style added a literary dimension. He raised Renault's consumer profile, as the R19 was aimed at customers with a high socio-cultural level. Le-Tan is known for the book covers that he has produced for the writer Patrick Modiano. They share the same world, the same talent for creating atmospheres with an indefinable charm which speak to our inner selves.

*Le roi Louis II de Bavière*

*L'heure des "drinks"*

calèche à Séville

Levens Hall

Les Jardins de l'Alhambra
à Grenade

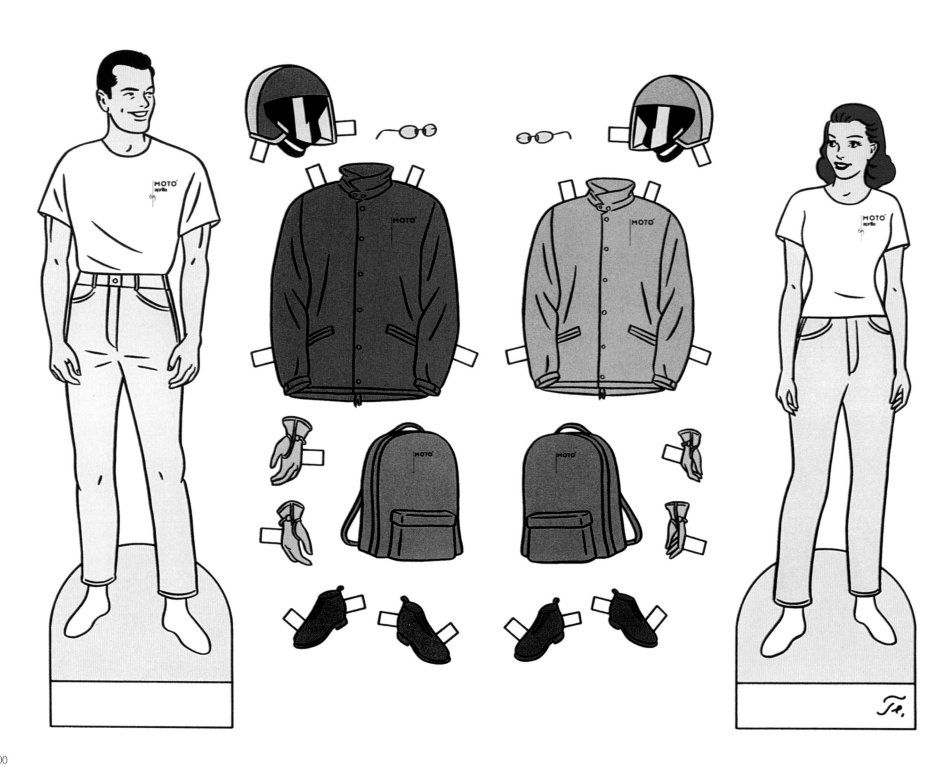

## A designer bike

The Moto' is a 650 cc motorbike designed by Philippe Starck for a sophisticated urban market. As it is not too heavy and both powerful and easy to handle, it appeals to men and women alike. We added these cut-out illustrations by Floc'h to the launch pack, a family photo album that showed Philippe Starck's friends depicted in black and white on the motorbike. Floc'h succeeded in reproducing the distinctive characteristics of this new urbanite down to the last detail. His clean lines established a feeling of ease and comfort that reflected the "easy-going" spirit of the motorbike. The parallel between the cut-out accessories and the biking clothes amusingly suggests an extremely fashionable locker room.

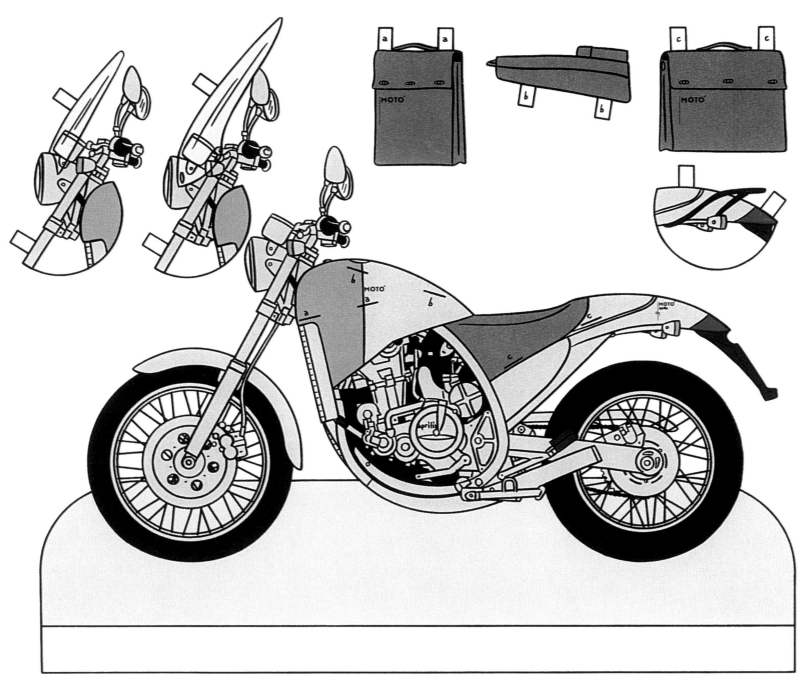

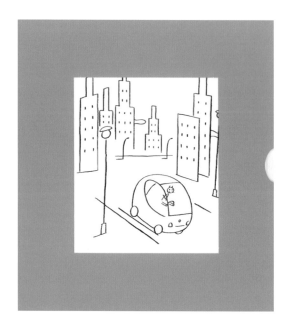

## The city in bloom

When the Twingo was dressed by Kenzo for a limited edition, it marked the meeting between two equally bright, invigorating and colourful viewpoints – Kenzo's "The world is beautiful" and Renault's "car for living". The result was the first designer Twingo.

The press pack we prepared for the launch was an attractive square book, with a meadow-green cover dotted with adhesive, cut-out flowers. It opened to reveal a pop-up with an illustration by Lorenzo Mattotti, who was inspired by the print on the seats to reinvent the giant poppy, Kenzo's fetish flower.

Using a drawing by Philippe Petit-Roulet, the illustrator who set the style for the Twingo advertising campaigns, we created a magic slate: a sliding

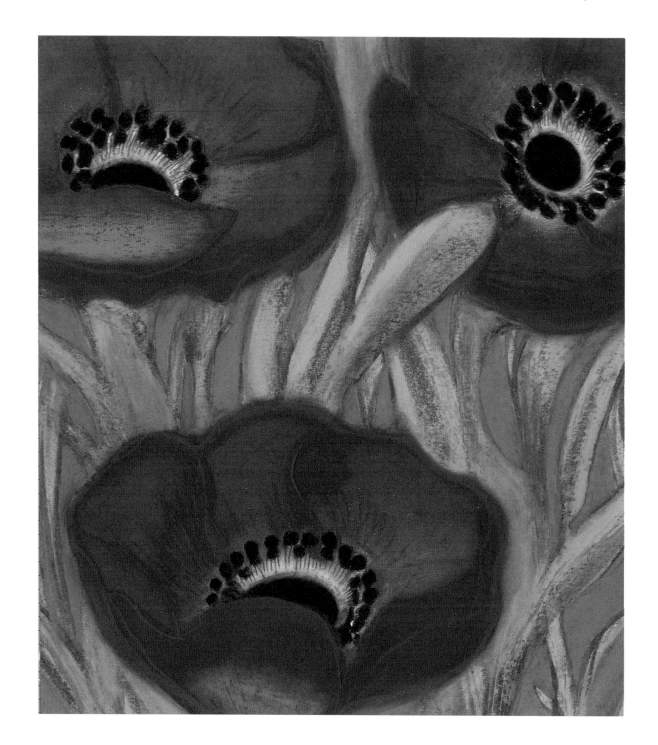

Philippe PETIT-ROULET
**Renault**
1995 - *Twingo Kenzo*

device converted the black drawing on a white background into a red car in a colourful city swathed in flowers. His apparently naive graphic style is remarkably effective, full of mischief and accessible to everyone. The already likeable-looking car gains even more vitality and charm.

# P A N N E   S È C H E

Sa Starfire en panne sèche à dix kilomètres de là, un autostoppeur arrive à la station Phillips 66. Il se nomme Ray Banana et a roulé une partie de la nuit, bien que ça ne se voie pas sur son visage. Alf, le pompiste, garde pimpante sa station située en plein désert Mojave, même si la route est de moins en moins fréquentée. Banana fait remplir son jerrycan et s'enquiert de ses chances de trouver une voiture allant vers l'est pour le ramener à son cabriolet. "Si vous êtes vraiment veinard, peut-être..." dit Alf.

"Je ne sais pas ce qui se passe, elles vont toutes vers l'ouest, ces derniers temps!"

Enfin, celles qui roulent. Cette Ford rose, là, ça n'est pas près de lui arriver.

Température: 100° Fahrenheit (38° centigrades).

Une Allard à la pompe. Est-ce que ça a un sens, Banana, de demander à un de ces sportsmen de faire dix kilomètres à rebrousse-poil et bousiller sa moyenne? Ces bagnoles-là, ça taille la route comme le fil coupe le beurre, sans regarder en arrière.

Au Ludlow Café, la gérante se dit qu'il est peut-être temps de débarrasser les restes du petit déjeuner. Et qu'attend-il donc ainsi au soleil, celui-là?

## A comic reinvented

When Jean-Michel Wilmotte was commissioned to decorate the interior of the Quick fast-food restaurant in Angoulême, the international capital of the comic book, he asked Ted Benoit to imbue it with his vision of the world. The walls were thus covered with huge frescoes featuring Ray Banana, the cartoonist's favourite character, a kind of crime-novel antihero who moves in a world inspired by California after World War II.

It seemed a shame not to publish these images. So, Ted Benoit came up with a story, *Panne sèche* (Dry Breakdown), which made use of all his preparatory drawings. We turned them into a poster measuring 120 x 170 cm, which was distributed to all Quick's customers during the three days of the Festival de la Bande Dessinée in 1990.

Ted BENOIT
Quick
1990 - Poster

Elle s'appelle Thelma Ritter, et elle a repris ce café après la mort tragique de son mari, Elmer. Elle aimerait que le moustachu ôte ses lunettes noires. Elle a un a priori contre les gens dont elle ne peut croiser le regard.

Schulz et O'Meara, les mécanos, découvrent que toute la segmentation du moteur de la Ford est à refaire. Ca semble bien les amuser. O'Meara a une collection de casquettes étonnante. Il en change trois fois par jour.

Alf vient s'en jeter une au frais du Ludlow Café, et essaie sa dernière blague sur Thelma qui l'écoute d'une oreille, songeant au moustachu: sera-t-il toujours là à la nuit?

"Bon sang, crie Banana, vu le peu de clients que vous avez, ça ne vous coûterait vraiment rien de prendre votre dépanneuse pour m'emmener à ma voiture!" Oui, mais...

...la dépanneuse est en panne. Ainsi va la vie dans le désert Mojave.

à
suivre...

Les chiens de prairie mettent le nez dehors. Alf fait ses comptes de la semaine, il n'y a rien à la télé. Dans son arrière-boutique Thelma hésite: dormir encore ici, ou prendre sa Chevrolet, garée derrière, pour rentrer à son appartement de Métropolis, où elle n'a pas mis les pieds depuis quinze jours?
Elle pourrait du même coup faire le détour pour déposer à sa voiture l'homme au jerrycan. D'accord, elle a pensé un moment qu'il avait une tête de gangster, mais à la réflexion il n'a pas l'air d'un mauvais bougre.

François AVRIL
**EDF**
*1993 - Rendre le sourire à la ville*

## Smile, you can breathe!

In the early 1990's, the research undertaken by EDF and its partners had taken the electric car to a level of technological maturity that made it a credible response to the environmental problems of modern cities. *Rendre le sourire à la ville* (Putting a Smile on the City) was a document aimed at the general public that sought to convey the advantages of electric traction.

To counterpoint the detailed arguments in the text, François Avril's breezy illustrations portrayed a utopian city, both quiet and unpolluted, where it would at last be possible to co-exist intelligently with cars. Trees, birds and babies can all thrive in its streets with a human face. The music floating out of the window is no longer drowned out by the roar of traffic. The poetic approach superseded all the rational arguments by submitting one simple piece of evidence: the city can breathe.

## The Var, land of adventure

How to interest the teenagers of the Var in discovering their region's heritage? This was the objective of *Var, le département dont vous êtes le héros* (Var, the département where you are the hero), a promotional album sponsored by the local authorities and set in motion by the Multicom agency.

The result was both a game and a comic book that spread its message like the branches of a tree. It offered readers a treasure hunt that they devised themselves and unfurled according to the choices and decisions they made. A team of specialists was on hand to lead them to the treasure: Jean-Luc Fromental, the scripter, and his accomplice, Floc'h, who had already published several comic books together. They were joined by François Nedelec, a specialist in role-playing games, who categorised all the possible situations by computer. At least three hours was needed to cover the whole book.

We produced an edition that was fairly ambitious – 28 x 34 cm landscape format, hardback cover, full-page illustrations – to give it all the attributes of a real book and exalt what was a truly innovative promotion on the part of a local authority. With a print run of 10,000 copies, it was distributed free in the secondary schools and colleges of the *département* and was awarded the Prize for the Best Promotional Use of a Comic Strip at the Angoulême Festival.

FLOC'H
Conseil général du Var
1989 - *Var, le département dont vous êtes le héros*

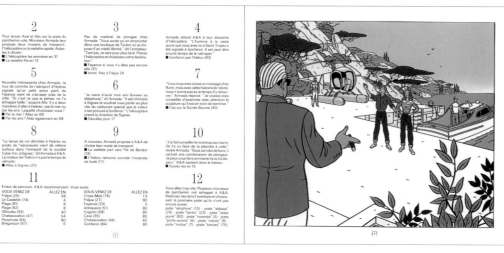

Yves CHALAND
**Conseil régional de Bretagne**
1990 - *Avis aux jeunes citoyens bretons*

## Go for it, lads!

The comic book was also the medium adopted by the Brittany Regional Council to make children aware of the dynamism of their region and its place in the new Europe. Yves Chaland was chosen as the illustrator and scripter, as his graphic world and clean drawing style guaranteed great accessibility among young readers.

Chaland made a research trip in spring 1990, and he had already finished the script, cut-outs and pencil sketches, as well as designing the cover image, when a terrible accident cost him his life on the holiday roads. Despite the shock, we had to hire someone else to take over, in order to fulfil our commitment to the Regional Council. His closest friends rallied round to bring his work to fruition. François Avril completed the drawings; Isabelle Beaumenay, Chaland's wife, handled the colouring and Jean-Luc Fromental came on board for the writing. Thanks to the energy of one and all, the work was finally printed. Just as it was about to be distributed, however, somebody in the upper reaches of the Regional Council spotted a spelling mistake which, despite multiple proof readings, had slipped into one of the speech bubbles on the cover (which had been written by Chaland himself). It had escaped the eyes of everyone, and 10,000 copies of the book had already been printed! We had no choice but to reprint the cover, unbind the book and put it back together – and, of course, accept the financial consequences. Despite this, we could not help seeing this as a wink from our friend in the great beyond. And the story of this comic book will remain a special memory for ever.

François AVRIL
**Conseil régional de Bretagne**
1990 - *Avis aux jeunes citoyens bretons*

Stanislas BARTHÉLÉMY
**Conseil régional de Bretagne**
1990 - *Avis aux jeunes citoyens bretons*

Fashion, ephemeral and desirable… Ethereal, it passes like a light breeze heralding the new season, but it has meaning because it reveals our own "fashions" of living and thinking at a particular moment. Fashion is a reflection of the times. In fashion we speak about style, and we also say that illustrators have a style of their own. The two were therefore made for each other.  Certain illustrators are in fashion. Others create it. They sketch it, paint it and unravel it. They suggest, highlight and send back to us a certain image of ourselves. Are they really talking about us, however, or about people whose reflection we would love to be ours? The apparent superficiality of the subject gives them a lightness of touch. This is what charms us and fills us with wonder.

# PUBLICITÉS

*Previous page:*

Serge CLERC
**ERGEE**
*1993 - Limited Edition*
Fifth collection, spring/summer

Jean-Philippe DELHOMME
**Le Bon Marché**
*2005 - 15 ans de création*

## How to be "Rive Gauche"

Since the LVMH group took over the Bon Marché in 1990, the store has been in permanent transformation. The year 2005 saw the completion of building works and a comprehensive refurbishment. To mark this stage and assess the progress in repositioning the store's image, the Communications department asked us to think about a prestige publication, aimed essentially at the editors of major French press outlets. Of the five proposals that we presented to Séverine Merle, the store's Image Director, the final choice went to a portfolio whose 30 x 40 cm format recalls the fully illustrated calendar published every year in a limited edition by Vue sur la Ville. In a soft box fastened by a band marked with the slogan "15 Years of Creation", seven themes were developed through photographs and texts, introduced on the cover by a full-page illustration. By then, Jean-Philippe Delhomme had been collaborating for some time with the store, notably in creating the small illustrated flyers with which Bon Marché was communicating with its clientele. He is internationally known for his collaborations with major fashion and interior design magazines, and for advertising campaigns in Japan and the USA, in particular for Volvo and Barneys. He is appreciated for his keen observations and evocative painting style, so descriptive of the attitudes of our time. He appeals to a young and informed public.

In order to capitalise on the understanding of tone and approach that he had already seemed to develop with Bon Marché, we asked him to do the illustrations for the portfolio: eight small scenes or situations which express a slightly bohemian Left-Bank spirit, characterised by culture, modernity and a selective approach to the art of living. It was a collaboration which did not have to stop there, because in 2006 the Bon Marché entrusted him with its image and poster campaign on the walls of the Paris Métro.

Jean-Philippe DELHOMME
**Le Bon Marché**
*2005 - 15 ans de création*

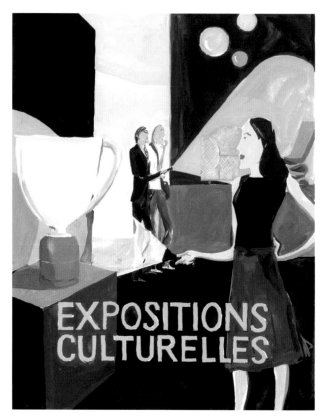

nouveaux
espaces

# amitié avec les créateurs

Jean-Philippe DELHOMME
**Le Bon Marché**
*2005 - 15 ans de création*

Michael ROBERTS
Chanel
1997 - *Les Signes d'identification instantanée de Chanel*

## A dream of luxury in tune with the times

The Crillon is not only one of the most prestigious luxury hotels in Paris, it is also a chic and convivial meeting place that benefits from a strategic location right in the heart of the city. Opening onto place de la Concorde, with its back to the Faubourg Saint-Honoré, it unites two of the capital's main tourist assets: History and Fashion. When Francka Holtmann took over the direction of the hotel, she asked us to reconsider its graphic identity and image. Among various projects, we worked on a Christmas card – a difficult exercise if ever there was one. Illustration makes it possible to circulate messages for this occasion without the need for words. First we had to find an appropriate style in which the recipients of the message would recognise themselves; then the paper, colours and form that would make them want to keep an intrinsically ephemeral creation for a lifetime.

Starting with the concept "the Hotel Crillon offers you all of Paris", we devised a card with a system of flaps hiding a fir tree decorated with the major Parisian monuments. We designed the general setting, the characters' poses and clothes – among others, dresses by Dior and Lanvin – and the principal elements of the decor. Marguerite Sauvage brought a sexy touch to a delicate, dreamlike world of luxury. The traditional aspect of the evening clothes was countered by the faces and the hairstyles, where the influence of manga culture could be glimpsed. The very fashionable tone is youthful and cosmopolitan – an image with which the Crillon's clientele is happy to identify itself.

Marguerite SAUVAGE
**Hôtel de Crillon**
2005 - 2006 Christmas card

## Chanel icons

It is rare for couture houses to bother with institutional PR. Press coverage obtained several times a year during fashion shows is usually considered sufficient to uphold their image. In deciding to produce a brochure on the *éléments d'identification instantanée de Chanel* (instant identification marks of Chanel; Karl Lagerfeld's formula), the company intended to capitalise on what gives Chanel its edge, on what it is that means that makes a creation by Chanel immediately recognisable, anywhere in the world, and never confused with any other.

Starting with the principal that Coco Chanel was her own model, we created a black silhouette in her image, like a shadow puppet, with a series of auto-adhesive complements that could be arranged in endless combinations. To show the variety of the designs, we filled drawing boards with several variations on the famous Chanel bag, the beige shoe with black toe, chains, buttons, costume jewellery and, of course, the camellia, the true icon of the house. Originally aimed exclusively at fashion editors, the success of this brochure was such that Chanel ordered 15,000 copies to be distributed to the clients of its European boutiques during the Christmas period. Young mothers gave them to their daughters. A clever idea for introducing the young generation to the world of Chanel.

## The geometry of realism

When the S. T. Dupont company asked us to produce a press pack to present the design of its new boutique for menswear and accessories, the store was still under construction. All we had to picture the new space and form an overall impression of the brand for men were the architect's plans and the index of the materials to be used: Zebrano wood, metal, steel and leather, with Terrazo stone on the floor. Marguerite Sauvage's drawings went well with the rather dry precision of the plans. The space, cut up and furnished in a sober and geometric manner, expresses a strong modernity. The young and extremely hip figures shown inside sum up the contemporary positioning of the brand. She succeeded in finding exactly the right visual look.

Marguerite SAUVAGE
**S.T. Dupont**
2004 - Press pack

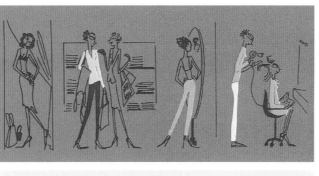

CARLOTTA
**Le Printemps**
1998 - Store guide

## "For the love of women"

In 1997, Printemps Haussmann was preparing for the reopening of the Nouveau Printemps de la Mode – five floors entirely rethought, renovated and devoted to fashion in all its forms. We thought long and hard about how to produce a guide presenting the overall feel of the store to give to visitors who came to discover it. It required a light and festive style that had to complement the spirit of the themes used for the opening – "la vie en rose" and "la femme-fleur" – as well as asserting the store's new slogan: "For the love of women". In order to depict the store's cheerful and busy atmosphere, we suggested a series of illustrations that would be published in the centre of the guide, in five strips one above the other, featuring a detailed presentation of the five floors. This is how the little world created by Carlotta took hold of Printemps. Her lively style, which combines humour and sophistication, has an exuberance perfectly suited to the store's new positioning. Carlotta sketches very Parisian attitudes with a light touch, and evokes a world that is lively and easy-going. Her quintessentially Parisian women delight the store's customers by transmitting a contemporary image that is bright and up-to-date. The various figures in different situations suggest the popularity and range of the merchandise on offer. We can see them being tempted, weighing things up, chatting, trying on clothes – in brief, a whole world that is essentially feminine. With her totally irresistible sketches, Carlotta provided a fashionable breath of fresh air and took us on a journey of discovery, pleasure and novelty.

CARLOTTA
**Le Printemps**
1998 - Store guide

## An exercise in style

Interpreting Printemps' 1997 Christmas card is an educational exercise in style. Here we find femininity, elegance, sensuality, colour, imagination, the store's dome metamorphosed into an evening dress, a woman's neck stretched like a glass bridge, five coloured feathers symbolising the five floors, day and night, luxury and beauty, and a thousand other things that each person may read into the image. The magic of illustration is its ability to sum up a world in a single image. Lorenzo Mattotti was in his element here. For many years, he has been interpreting the fashion of the great couturiers for *Vanity* magazine. The store's image can only benefit from the work of such an artist. Dealing in wonder always brings rewards.

Lorenzo MATTOTTI
**Le Printemps**
1997 - Christmas card

1. Yves CHALAND
2. FLOC'H
3. Walter MINUS
4. Serge CLERC
5. Ted BENOIT
6. Pierre CLÉMENT
**Ergee**
1990 - *Limited Edition*
First collection, autumn/winter

1

## The sock dips its toes into comics

Our collaboration with the German sock manufacturer Ergee, via its PR agency Avantgarde (later Start Advertising), proved to be a real adventure in itself: a serial in six episodes where a team of cartoonists, spurred on by the pleasure of working together, expressed their creativity while accepting constraints that were to say the least unusual in their working practice. One day in 1990, we received a visit at Vue sur la Ville from a young advertising executive from Munich, Claudia Langer. One of her clients was Ergee, a large manufacturer of socks and tights, who needed, on the one hand, to rejuvenate their rather staid image and, on the other, to develop new lines for men. French comic books represented the height of modernity to this young and dynamic agency, in tune with current trends. She therefore imagined the reproduction of characters or scenes from comics as jacquard motifs on a new collection of socks to be produced in a limited edition. The operation would be accompanied by a PR campaign aimed at the press and in-store promotional material. The agency asked us to give the project style and coherence by making the meeting between these two worlds plausible. We would choose a theme for each new season that would be developed by several cartoonists and presented to the press in the form of a generic image, then developed in several motifs on a line of socks to be baptised *Limited Edition* (15,000 pairs

2

Ladies and a gentleman

3

4

5

PORTRAIT OF THE ARTIST AS A PRIVATE EYE.

6

FLOC'H
Ergee
1990 - *Limited Edition*
First collection,
autumn/winter

227

1. Walter MINUS
2. Serge CLERC
3. Pierre CLÉMENT
4. Yves CHALAND
**Ergee**
1991 - *Limited Edition*
Second collection, spring/summer

3

1

2

4

were produced). Our accomplices were six of the best emerging or confirmed talents of the moment: Yves Chaland, Floc'h, Ted Benoit, Serge Clerc, Walter Minus and Pierre Clément.

A special edition would serve as a springboard for the press launch of the operation: the most important journalists would receive a numbered and signed silkscreen print of an illustration, one of just 400 copies. It was produced by Floc'h, who portrayed an elegant couple, her in an evening dress, him in a dinner jacket and … socks standing on the ledge of the fountain in place de la Concorde. In order to establish right away the spirit of *Limited Edition*, we maintained the "comic-strip" style as the unifying theme for the first season. For the in-store promotional material, we asked each illustrator to produce a postcard from which we would extract a graphic element that could be reproduced as a motif on the socks. Going to the factory to see the transition from drawing to finished product, we discovered to our horror that the production line was not computer-driven. Each illustrator had to redo his drawing on squared paper so that it could be adapted to the weft of the jacquard loom.

Six months later, for the following collection, we continued the same theme. Each illustrator gave free rein to his inspiration and style. Everything was done with good humour. The product was attractive and we were there to make it playful and surprising. The illus-

1

1 and 4. FLOC'H
2. Ted BENOIT
3. Serge CLERC
**Ergee**
1991 - *Limited Edition*
Third collection, autumn/winter

2

3

4

trators adapted willingly to the technical constraints. In exchange, we made sure that the execution was as respectful of their work as possible.

## All round the world

To take full advantage of the idea of postcards, the third collection revolved around travel. The generic image of the press pack, again produced by Floc'h, was a cardboard disc, designed to be suspended from store ceilings, which released an accordion-style gatefold of tourist postcards. Each illustrator was to choose whichever country he liked best.

At that moment, however, Yves Chaland was suddenly killed in an accident. So that he would always be with us in the venture, we adapted one of his drawings, in agreement with his wife Isabelle Beaumenay.

1

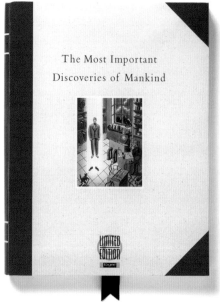

## The great inventions

The following season, Loustal joined us. By now, the concept had evolved, and, for the first time, a text accompanied the images. It was to be iconoclastic, in the spirit of a comic book. The subject was a review of the great discoveries of humanity. The press pack was contained in a beautiful box, like an ancient manuscript. On the cover, in miniature at the bottom of the box, Loustal drew a character in a laboratory, on a stormy night, sucked up by a magnetic phenomenon. His shoes stay on the ground, but he is levitated, in his socks of course. Inside the box was a stack of six four-page documents, in which each artist illustrated a fundamental discovery which – before the invention of men's socks – changed the face of the world. Floc'h chose Gutenberg and printing; Ted Benoit, Galileo; Pierre Clément, the wheel; Walter Minus, space; Serge Clerc Archimedes and the Greek philosophers, and Loustal, fire. The project started to grow in size: the following season we proposed that each illustrator take on the personality of a musician or singer in the musical world with which he felt the most affinity. These illustrations appeared in shops on fake record covers.

EPPVR', SI MVOVE!

TED·BENOIT

2

1 and 4. LOUSTAL
2. Ted BENOIT
3. FLOC'H
5. Pierre CLÉMENT
6. Serge CLERC
**Ergee**
1992 - *Limited Edition*
Fourth collection, spring/summer

Young Gutenberg.

3

4

5

6

1. Walter MINUS
**Ergee**
1993 - *Limited Edition*
Fifth collection, autumn/winter

2. Serge CLERC
**Ergee**
1993 - *Limited Edition*
Fifth collection, autumn/winter

## Greatest hits

As had happened every season, the motifs on the socks echoed an element from the drawing. "Comic socks meet music" announced the press release, in the form of a record cover. Inside, on real vinyl, there was a compilation of different musical styles, and all the record covers appeared with a blurb on the particular musician-illustrator written by Jean-Luc Fromental, in the style of the specialist music critics. That year, we had the pleasure of seeing this work pick up the "Alph'art" award at the Angoulême Festival, the prize for the best use of comic art in an advertising campaign.

1. Pierre CLÉMENT
2. LOUSTAL
3. FLOC'H
4. Walter MINUS
**Ergee**
1993 - *Limited Edition*
Fifth collection, autumn/winter
Text: Jean-Luc Fromental


*Following pages:*

1. Ted BENOIT
2. Walter MINUS

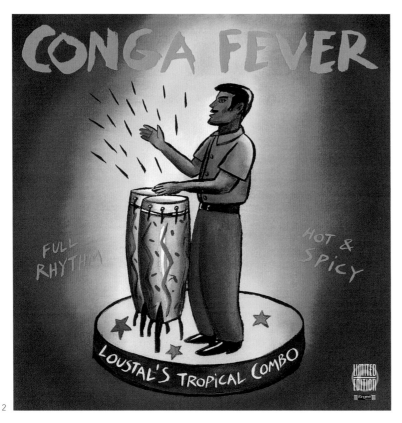

## TED BENOIT
*King of the blues*

Of the two nicknames given to him by his peers, Ted "Chalk Face" or "Twelve Finger" Benoit has always preferred the second. Nevertheless, if the virtuosity of his playing classes him indisputably among the Greats, on a par with Big Bill Broonzy or Blind Lemon Jefferson, it is the colour of his skin that has made him a legend. How a pasty-white frog came to croon his despair with as much conviction as the dark sons of the South will remain forever a mystery of modern musicology. Because, as this compilation of his rarest recordings proves, old "Chalk Face" truly was and will ever be a "King of the blues".

## FLOC'H
*Manhattan Romance*

The maestro raises his baton and the champagne begins to flow… So much joy and nostalgia, so many suave memories of an era never to return are woven through the fourteen tracks of this essential "best of" that the throat tightens as soon as the needle touches the first groove. The women were more gorgeous in those days, and their kisses were softer. Night fell over Manhattan as it sparkled like a diamond necklace. Cooing lovers left the ballroom of a thousand lights and walked into a night star-studded with crystalline notes to murmur their promises of eternal love. It was a time before the gangs, the golden boys and Trump Tower… Floc'h and his big band played their "effervescent music" and the whole of America fizzed.

## WALTER & MINUS
*My heart "beast" faster when I see you*

Fans of all ages, get read to cheer, 'cos they're back. We're talking about the inimitable "Three Fs" ("funny, furious and furry"), the most celebrated cat 'n' dog duo of them all: Walter & Minus. After "No Dogs Attached", "Real Cats Don't Bark" and "Catnip Madness", this new compilation takes the original soundtrack of their twelve latest films. Fifty minutes of pure madness awaits. But seriously, this LP marks a real testament as the W&M press office has just announced that Laurent L. Chartreux, the irreplaceable "voice" of Minus the cat, has decided to leave the magical world of cartoons to devote himself entirely to his career as a crooner.

## LOUSTAL
*Conga fever*

Anyone who associates island music with bad dress sense should look no further than this impeccable combo who never use the sweltering tropical heat as an excuse to give in to sloppy dressing. From the shine in their boots to the sharpness of their brilliantined quiffs, Señor Loustal's guys offer an image of the Caribbean that is at last worthy of a fashion plate. And one could say the same for their music, whose rhythms are as feverish as most of us can take, and encourage an elegant swaying of the hips without bringing on an epileptic fit. Under the iron rod of their *leader massimo*, a hard taskmaster if ever there was one, this combo can swing all night long without ever creasing your shirt.

## SERGE CLERC
*A girl like this*

Hot and bop are deconstructed to the point of madness by the caustic reeds of the Clerc Quartet. Heady as a rainy Sunday on Christopher Street, ghostly as a funeral cortège climbing Lenox Avenue in a backwards march, this unfettered jazz, under the constraints of "free", which some poisoned pens and small-minded critics have dared to call "nothing more than wild imaginings", exhale at full lung capacity the putrid air of the real New York. "Mutilating the standards is a sacred mission," declared the great Clerc in a recent interview. "I'm the Frankenstein of jazz. Hand me an old Bird improv, a Miles riff and I will reconstruct the little guy from start to finish. It's rickety as hell, OK, but cool man, very cool!"

## GNÄDIGERSTEIN
*Mäusetotenlieder*

What is a "sistrum", musical novices may ask. This modest percussion instrument composed of a curved square crossed by several moveable and sounding rods, whose origins go back to ancient Egypt, plays a crucial role in the score of the Mäusetotenleider, as it is this instrument that is has the onerous task of interpreting the theme of the mouse which occurs throughout the work. The admirable virtuosity of the sistrier Pierre Clément here makes all the difference, and places this nineteenth recorded version of Gnädigerstein's Magnum Opus far above the eighteen others recorded to this day.

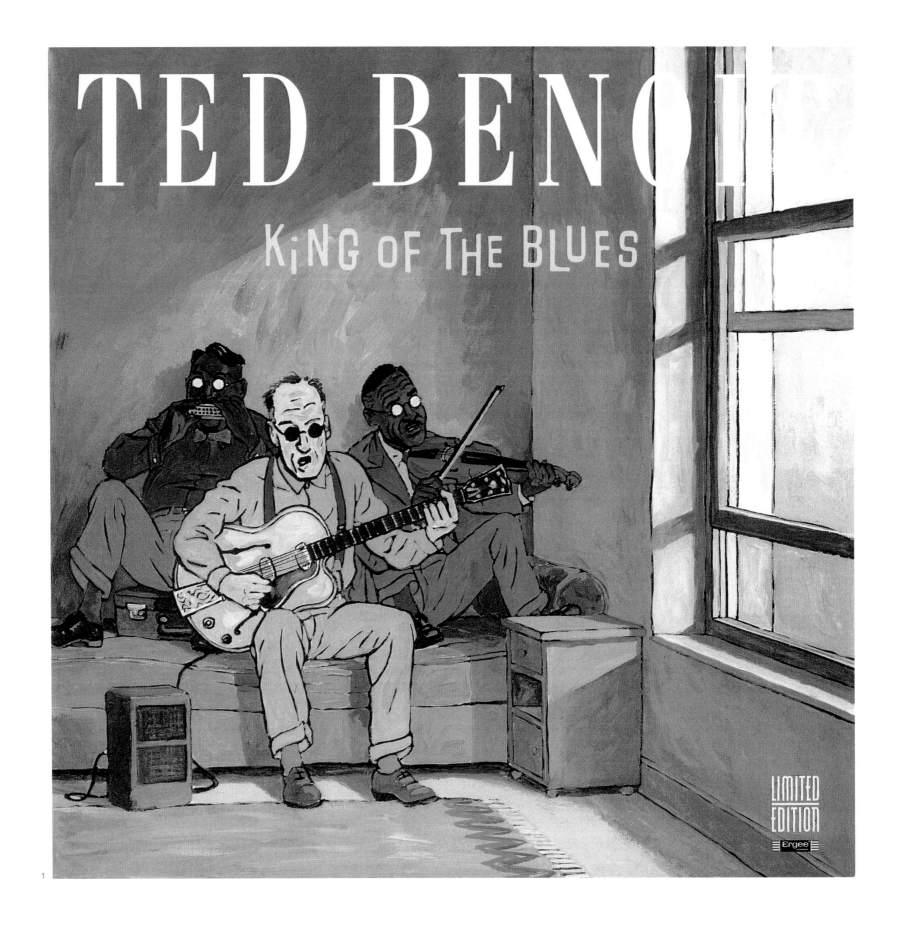

# Qui a tué
## Leonid Epsilon?

### SANG AU MUSÉE!
### Le corps du sarcophage défie la police!

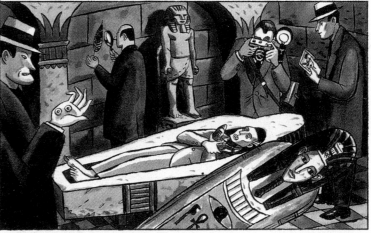

*Photo: Loustal*

**Un roman policier en six chaussettes!**

Avec sa sixième Limited Edition, Ergee part sur les traces des maîtres du mystère, Sherlock Holmes, Hercule Poirot, Maigret. Mais ce sont les chaussettes qui racontent l'histoire!

Six starts de la bande dessinée ont conçu puor Ergee six motifs de ces personnages avait une bonne raison d'assassiner le géant de la presse Leonid Epsilon, retrouvé mort dans d'étranges circonstances. Mais qui des six est coupable? Qui est innocent?

Si vous découvrez la clé du mystère, vous pourrez gagner un voyage à Paris et de nombreux autres prix (voir dernière page).

Tous les éléments permettant de résoudre l'énigme se trouvent dans ce récit.

Alors, espèrons que vos deux pieds ont d'excellents alibis...

Paris - Hier 21 mars, après la fermeture, des gardiens du musée du Louvre ont découvert dans une salle peu fréquentée le corps de Leonid Epsilon, le géant de la presse. Leonid Epsilon reposait, pieds nus, dans un sarcophage égyptien. Une lame aiguë lui avait cisaillé le bulbe rachidien. Son sternum présentait une fracture. Il avait en poche la photo d'un tableau. Près du sarcophage reposaient deux yeux de verre arrachés à un ours en peluche, et une plume de perroquet. Malgré le nombre des indices, l'enquête s'annonce très délicate.

Tragique ironie du sort, la vie d'Epsilon se clôt par l'un de ces meurtres sensationnels qui assurèrent avec le reportage d'investigation le succès de ses journaux.

Né à Istamboul en 1930, Epsilon eut une jeunesse tumultueuse, devint reporter à «France-Soir» et claqua la porte six mois plus tard pour fonder sa propre agence de presse, Alpha-Epsilon. D'abord sise au 21h rue Auguste-Dupin, en plein Saint-Germain-des-Prés, où Epsilon résidait alors, l'agence devint le pivot d'un puissant groupe international. La clé du succès d'Epsilon fut le talent avec lequel il savait faire partager ses passions aux autres.

Hemingway lui avait donné le virus des taureaux. Alors que la corrida était ignorée, Epsilon ajouta une page tauromachique aux éditions de son quotidien européen «Alpha-Tribune». Le public s'enthousiasma! L'art fut l'autre raison de vivre d'Epsilon. Tournant le dos au cubisme, il promut dans ses pages une peinture accessible à tous. Il imposa le genre «figuratif colonial» et ses nus africains naïfs, dont il fut un grand collectionneur.

Homme séduisant et comblé ses conquêtes ne se comptaient pas Leonid Epsilon menait depuis peu une vie très retirée. Il meurt sans laisser d'héritier connu.

*(correspondance particulière)*

1. FLOC'H
2. Walter MINUS
3. Ted BENOIT
4. Serge CLERC
5. LOUSTAL
6. Pierre CLÉMENT
**Ergee**
1993 - *Limited Edition*
Sixth collection, spring/summer
Text: François Landon

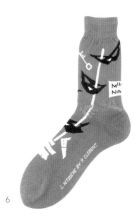

1      2      3      4      5      6

### RONALD & DONALD MACBIRDIE

These eccentric twins are well known in high society. Where does their love of birds come from? From the name of their Scottish ancestors, whose castle in the Highlands they bought back? From the time when they performed a hypnotism number with intelligent birds in the casinos of Cairo? The MacBirdies know a lot about a lot of people. Too much, perhaps… Is this the source of their fortune? Their paths had crossed with that of Leonid Epsilon and not much love was lost between them…

### MARIE-FRANCE LEBRUN

Why does this stunning woman surround herself with teddy bears? Doesn't she believe that her beauty could conquer anyone? These days she lives an uneventful life on the Côte d'Azur. It is a long time since she left Versailles, cutting all links with her family, interrupting her studies to embark on a new existence… Is Marie-France Lebrun too much of a woman to be honest? How did she know Leonid Epsilon? Did the newspaper baron discover the secret she was keeping? And who else knows her secret?

### PAUL HOWLETT

Could there be anything more ordinary than being an English teacher in Versailles? But what if that teacher had previously been a toreador in Mexico, with so much talent that Picasso devoted a series of sketches to him… And what if he had married the daughter of a a great English art patron, and was still married to her… What, too, if a scandal had forced him to change his name and nationality… And what if he was paying for a moment of weakness with a life in front of the blackboard… What if he feared that reporters would discover, under his new identity, traces of the exceptional toreador he once was… But aside from Leonid Epsilon, which newspaper chief is interested in bull-fighting?

### LEO MELIKIAN

Fans of Cubism admire this dandy, charming and persuasive art dealer who is a Picasso specialist. Leo Melikian's personality is as passionate and explosive as the canvases that fascinate him. He divides his life between his Versailles mansion and his Parisian gallery in Saint-Germain-des-Près. But business is not going well for him. In the paintings market, the art he loves has been superseded by the figurative colonial style. For the art dealer, one person is responsible for the ruin that threatens him, the man who launched the style that Melikian abhors, Leonid Epsilon!

### ALBERT VANDEKOUKKE

Albert Vandekoukke has been thrown out of paradise. A customs officer in the Congo, he spent his time painting naïve-style nudes of African women… and trafficking crocodile skins and diamonds between there and Egypt. Discovered and dismissed, he left Africa. What was it that pushed him to sell his only treasure, his collection of paintings, for a mouthful of bread? Today he vegetates in an attic room in Paris's rue Dupin. He doesn't paint any more. Does he want to get back at the people who forced him to sell his works? Or the person who made them famous and still owns them all, the press baron Leonid Epsilon?

### LUCIE NITOUCHE

Grey and tiny like a mouse, Lucie Nitouche is but a silhouette behind the curtains of her concierge lodge, in a Parisian apartment block on the rue Dupin. A young woman who delivers the post and polishes the staircase… But how many other names has she? How many other faces? How many masks? How many conquests? Lucie Nitouche likes her life of perpetual disguise. Would she wipe out anyone who uncovered her secrets? She was young when Leonid Epsilon and his newspaper agency left rue Dupin. Why does she say she was the last woman that the press baron ever loved?

FLOC'H
alias R&D MacBirdie

## Who killed Leonid Epsilon?

The idea behind the next collection was to produce a small, tabloid-style 16-page newspaper in a 31 x 23 cm format, revolving around an illustrated crime story written by François Landon, with a corresponding competition for the public. The reader was invited to lead the investigation to discover which of the six characters concocted by each of the cartoonists is the murderer of a certain Leonid Epsilon. The clues were hidden in the illustrations of the text and motifs that appear on the socks, and everyone who bought a pair was offered a miniature comic-book version of the story. Once again, we were rewarded with the "Alph'art" prize for communication at Angoulême. This adventure was coming to its end, however. Another collection was produced, illustrated by Floc'h alone, on the principle of three-part gags, then one more, carried out by Serge Clerc. But that was the swansong. Ergee socks evolved towards other concepts, and it was time for us to move on to other things.

RONALD & DONALD MacBIRDIE

Ted BENOIT
alias Paul Howlett

Serge CLERC
alias Leo Malikian

PAUL HOWLETT

LÉO MELIKIAN

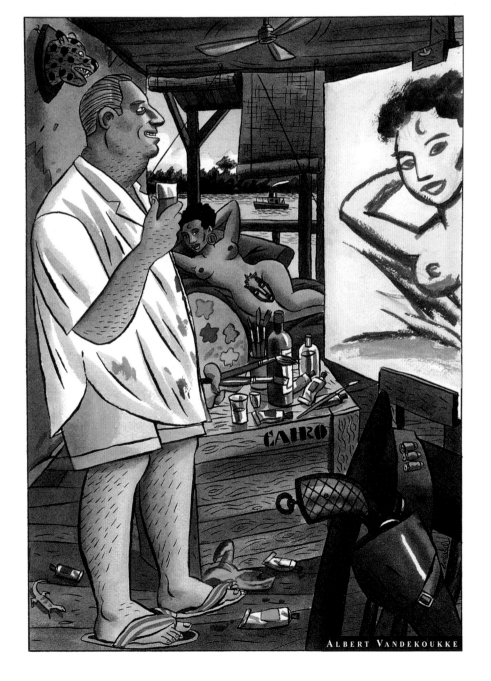

ALBERT VANDEKOUKKE

LUCIE NITOUCHE

Walter MINUS
alias Marie-France Lebrun

This experience over many years was fundamental for me and for Vue sur la Ville, which knew how to respond fully to its calling: to be a publishing house with a team of authors where each one is known, recognised and respected for his or her talent. Respect for the client and respect for the artists: that, if you like, is my creed. It is also a question of intellectual honesty. Never promise what you can't deliver, don't invent impossible hypotheses; otherwise, the illustrators can feel ill at ease or, even worse, betrayed. That is why we are very concerned about the quality of the projects we produce. The paper, the printing and the precise shades of the colours are all of primary importance. We must also stay realistic and never lose sight of the fact that we are dealing with applied art. We are charged with a mission. We have an obligation to our clients to produce results. This is the only way that we can instil the confidence that produces lasting relationships.

# INDEX & BIOGRAPHIES by Guillaume Frauly

## Ruben ALTERIO

Ruben Alterio, a painter, illustrator, author and decorator born in Argentina to artist parents, studied fine art in Buenos Aires before settling in France, where he has lived for many years. His dreamlike style – diluted colours and hazy pastel tones, reminiscent of watercolours – suits the world of fashion in many ways, and his many collaborations with great couturiers such as Christian Lacroix or Oscar de la Renta have attracted great attention. His rich imagination and graceful figures have equally charmed the world of the stage, as he has created the sets and costumes for several plays, operas and ballets, such as Nicolas Le Riche's choreography for the Ballet de Nancy in 2001 and *Don Quixote*, choreographed by Marie-Claude Pietragalla for the Marseilles Opera in 2003. He has also collaborated with René de Ceccatty and, above all, with his friend and compatriot the director Alfredo Arias, for whom he illustrated *Peines de cœur d'une chatte française* in 1990 and *Le Père Noël du siècle* in 1997 (Seuil Jeunesse). He recently illustrated the CD cover for the musical fable *La Belle et les Bêtes* (Heyoka Jeunesse/Actes Sud-Papiers). We can also credit him for several window displays at Galeries Lafayette, in 1997 and 2003. His works figure in numerous public and private collections and have been exhibited all over the world.
Pages: 37, 43

## François AVRIL

Born in Paris in 1961, François Avril is a comic artist, painter and illustrator. After studying at the National School of Applied Arts in Paris, he published his first comic book with Jean-Claude Götting, *Le Chemin des Trois Places* (Futuropolis, 1989). Next came *Le Voleur de ballerines* (Carton, 1986, republished by Albin Michel in 2004) written by Yann, Yves Chaland's favourite scripter. Chaland, moreover – with Avril's full approval – covered a whole page of the book with scribbles and ink, although only a few close friends were in on the joke. Next, Les Humanoïdes Associés published *Soirs de Paris*, a wordless comic book, this time in collaboration with Philippe Petit-Roulet. While the majority of Avril's

books have been produced by small publishers like Le Neuvième Monde or Alain Beaulet, his great comeback to comics came via the Dupuis publishing house. He has created numerous limited editions of signed screen prints, drawing primarily on cities like Tokyo, New York and Paris for inspiration. Much appreciated in Japan and the United States, he now contributes to numerous magazines, including *The New Yorker*, *Cosmopolitan*, *Ginza* (Japon), *Atmosphères*, *Libération* and *Lire*. François Avril also illustrates record covers. He has taken part in many advertising campaigns, for clients such as BNP, Danone, Vivendi and EDF. Long recognised as a painter, he exhibits regularly in Paris, Tokyo, Brussels and Geneva. He is the president and founder of the Le Crayon, an association of book, press and advertising illustrators. He lives in Paris, near Montmartre, with his wife, the illustrator Dominique Corbasson, and their three daughters.
Pages: 58, 80, 110, 128, 129, 142, 150, 160-167, 190, 196, 197, 206, 207, 210, 211

## Stanislas BARTHÉLÉMY

Born in Rennes in 1961, Stanislas Barthélémy is a comic artist, illustrator and author. After studying interior decoration at the School of Applied Arts in Paris, he launched the series *Victor Levallois* with Laurent Rullier; he was discovered in 1984 through his contributions to the fanzines *Électrode*, *Recto-Verso* and *Le Lynx à Tifs*, which was edited by Jean-Christophe Menu. A child of the Clear Line and an avid reader of the adventures of Blake and Mortimer, he continued to develop his favourite character, *Hector Gaulois*, while working for the fanzines *Cholestérol*, *Gabor Kao*, *Gargouille* and *PLG*. He has published works such as *La Grande Course* (1986) and *Le Pigeon* (1988) with Futuropolis, and *Toutinox raconte* (PMJ "Libre Court", 1995), *Homme-Autruche* (1998) and *Les Vies d'Hector Gaulois* (2003) with L'Association, of which he was one of the founder members. He also wrote *Trafic en Indochine* (Alpen Publishers, 1990) and was one of the authors of the comic biography of Hergé published in 1996. He collaborates on children's

books – *Demain, on lève l'ancre* by Pascal Garnier (Nathan, 2002), *Petits Lolos et Gros Soucis* by Amélie Cantin (Milan, 2002), *Le Bossu de la Bonne Mère* by Marc Séassau (Lito, 2003), *Je suis un héros: quatre aventures de Serge T.* by Marie-Aude Murail (Bayard, 2006) – and regularly draws cartoons for two titles from Bayard Presse, *J'aime lire* and *Je bouquine*.
Page: 211

## Bertrand BATAILLE

Born in Paris, the illustrator and poster designer Bertrand Chauveau alias Bertrand Bataille studied at the National Vocational School of Art, from which he graduated in 1971. He has designed posters for cultural events – the Cannes Film Festival in 1985, and the Amiens International Film Festival in 1993 – and also for films, including Philippe Muyl's *Cuisine et Dépendances*, in 1993. His dreamlike style has graced advertising campaigns for brands such as Schlumberger, Gan or Sopra, and he has collaborated with publishers such as France Loisirs and Robert Laffont. He has illustrated several books, including *La Danse des mots*, *Les Fables de La Fontaine*, *Nostalgies*, *Les Aventures du poisson volant* (Lito), *Objectif Gutta-Percha* by Freddy Woets (Lito, 2003) and, more recently, with – among others – the comic artist Martin Jarrie, *Contes des Amériques* (Lito, 2005), scripted by Ann Rocard.
Pages: 42, 43

## Glen BAXTER

Born in Leeds in 1944, Glen Baxter lives and works in London. He studied painting at art school in the early 1970s. His style – crosshatched line drawings in Indian ink and soft lead pencil, always captioned with plays on words that often revolve around food – has made him a master of nonsense and British humour. His stories are absurd and extravagant, and the graphic style echoes that of the novels published for teenagers between the two world wars. *Atlas*, his first book, was published in 1979 by De Harmonie and reissued by Thames & Hudson in 1983. A great comic illustrator, his heroes – cowboys, gauchos, phlegmatic cricket players and students in blazers – get a regular

airing in magazines such as *Vogue*, *The New Yorker*, *Le Nouvel Observateur*, *Le Monde* and *The New York Times*. As an illustrator and designer, he has designed frescoes for the Hôtel Windsor in Nice and, in 1999, he was commissioned to design a tapestry on the life of Richard the Lionheart by the French National Centre of Engraving and the Printed Arts. His books include *Glen Baxter Returns to Normal* (1992), *Glen Baxter's Gourmet Guide* (1997), *Trundling Grunts* (2002), *Blizzards of Tweed* (2003) and, most recently, *Loomings over the Suet* (2004), all published by Bloomsbury. His work has been exhibited at the Pompidou Centre in Paris, the Victoria and Albert Museum and the Tate Gallery in London, as well as in New York, San Francisco, Munich, Tokyo and Sydney.
Page: 111

## BEN RADIS

A comic scripter and artist born in Perreux in 1956, Rémi Bernardi, known as Ben Radis, began a short-lived career as a civil servant with the PTT (the French post, telecommunications and broadcasting service). He got interested in comics shortly afterwards and, in 1980, with Dominique Nicol, alias Dodo, he published his first drawings in the magazine *Métal hurlant*. Over six episodes they invented the saga of the *Closh*, an unhinged parody of a rock group. In 1983, with the appearance of *La nuit porte conseil*, the detective Gomina was born. The following year, he contributed to *Best*, a monthly rock magazine, before returning to *Métal hurlant* with new characters: Teddy, Billy and Zao. In 1987, Albin Michel published his *Le Point du jour*. He attracted attention in 1991, with the publication of *Bonjour les Indes*, an exploration of the world of travellers, hallucinogens and gurus (La Sirène). Ben Radis has also illustrated numerous record and CD covers with his style "somewhere between early Walt Disney and the Clear Line".
Page: 109

## Ted BENOIT

Thierry Benoit, known as Ted Benoit, was born in Niort in 1947. An author, comic artist and illustrator, he began his career as a scriptwriter after study-

ing film at the IDHEC in Paris. It was not until in 1971, when he was discovered by the famous American underground cartoonist Robert Crumb, that he turned to comic books and emerged as the natural successor to Hergé. He worked for the magazine *Geranonymo* and published his first strips in *L'Écho des Savanes* in 1975, before his first book, *Hôpital*, was published by Humanoïdes Associés; it won him the prize for Best Scenario at the Angoulême Festival in 1979. Inspired by the *film noir* of the 1950s and 60s, Benoit is the author of *Vers la ligne claire* (Les Humanoïdes Associés, 1981), in which the surrealist hero Ray Banana appeared for the first time, and *Berceuse électrique* (Casterman, 1982). He has published numerous illustrations in the magazines *À suivre*, *Libération* and *Domino*, as well as in *Le Figaro*. In 1993, the publisher Dargaud chose him to relaunch the adventures of Blake and Mortimer, taking over from Edgar P. Jacobs. The two mythical heroes reappeared in *L'Affaire Francis Blake* (1996) and *L'Étrange rendez-vous* (1996), still scripted by Jean Van Hamme. Continuing the tradition established by Jacobs, the two pals moved through a mixture of past and present. These books alternated with others drawn by the equally talented André Juillard. Ted Benoit regularly puts his stamp on advertising campaigns for Jameson whiskey, as well as for Shell, Kodak, Otis, Bic and Fiat. These days, he has returned to cinema and is working on a script for a feature film.
Pages: 204, 205, 226, 229, 231, 236, 239, 241

## BENOIT

The Flemish painter, illustrator, author and comic artist Benoît Van Innis, known as Benoit, was born in Bruges in 1960 and is one of the most important Belgian artists of his generation. He studied at the National School of Painting and Fine Arts in Ghent, where he teaches today. He began his career in magazines: *De Morgen*, *Panorama*, *de Volkskrant* in Belgium and the Netherlands, and *The New Yorker* in the United States. He also works for the French press: *Lire*, *Le Magazine littéraire*, *Le Nouvel Observateur*, *L'Expansion*, *VSD* and *Paris Match*,

alternating with Sempé, who discovered him. Throughout his published work he casts a sharp and caustic look at everyday life through his naive but often disconcerting characters. His minimalist style and corrosive humour won him a Silver Hat award at the International Festival of Comic Illustration at Knokke-Heist in 1987. He is the author of several books: *Rire en automne à Bruges* (Éditions Bernard Barrault, 1989), *Le Musée interdit* (Magic-Strip, 1990), *Le Vent est bleu* (Denoël), *Oncle Gilbert* (Seuil, 1995), *Hop-Hop la grenouille* (Albin Michel Jeunesse, 2005, with Axel Scheffler). In recent years, he has chosen to branch out into other media, such as the ceramic tiles he used for the Brussels Metro station of Maelbeek (2001) and the Jan Breydel football stadium in Bruges, where he created immense tiled frescoes. He lives and works in Brussels.
Pages: 30, 62, 94-96, 104, 105, 107, 115, 120, 121, 131, 188, 189, 195

## Christian BINET

Born in Tulle in 1947, Christian Binet saw his first drawing published in *Humour Magazine* in 1961 – when he was only 14. After drawing comics for the *Bulletin municipal d'Étampes* in 1967, he attended architecture school but comics were still his first love. The creator of the soldier Schwartz, who he invented for the army journal *TAM*, and, in 1975, of *Poupon la Peste*, Binet has been published in *Jours de France*, *Record* and *Formule 1*. Though he produced his first comics for adults in the fanzine *Mormoil* in 1974, he was only really discovered in 1977 with his first contribution to the magazine *Fluide glacial*, where he created Kador, the only dog ever known to read Kant, and his inimitable stereotyped masters Robert and Raymonde, *Les Bidochon*. His trademarks are black humour, irony and mockery and naive, wily and often pathetic characters. He presents the worst possible image of the French and they lap it up! Nineteen titles were to follow. Apart from this, he has published around 30 books, including *L'Institution*, which takes a swipe at religion and education, *Monsieur le Ministre*, books featuring Lucien Grandgarçon that pour scorn on politicians, and *Forum*, a less virulent but no less effective critique of French society. He is a *Chevalier* of the French Order of Arts and Letters.
Page: 108

## Serge BLOCH

Serge Bloch likes to call himself a comic artist rather than an illustrator. He is a social chronicler who, theatrically and humorously, plays with everyday icons and language while creating characters and concepts as vehicles to convey messages. Born in Colmar in 1956, Bloch studied decorative arts in Strasbourg, where the illustrator Claude Lapointe was his tutor. He quickly realised that he preferred ideas and symbols to style, his characteristic line to colour. He has increasingly mixed drawing and photography to create improbable situations. By staying in touch with his inner child, Bloch has learnt to unlearn much of what he was taught. He has a curious collection of items connected with the eyes. He is the editor of the magazine *Astrapi* and a member of the UBU (European Cartoon Association). As well as being the author of the series *Max et Lili*, published by Calligram, he has produced several children's books, including the series *Vive la grande école* ("Histoires" collection, Casterman), *Mon prof est un espion*, *La Porte ouverte* ("Romans" collection, Casterman) and *Moi j'attends…* with Davide Cali (Sarbacane, 2005).
Page: 81

## Gilles BOOGAERTS

Born in Paris in 1951, Gilles Boogaerts entered the Duperré Applied Arts School in 1967 and graduated in fashion illustration and textiles in 1972. He immediately started working as a freelance illustrator and was responsible for several textile designs for the great fashion designers of the time, such as Kenzo and Cacharel. In 1980, he founded Magic Studio, a company producing printed fabrics, and worked as its artistic director for four years. The following decade was devoted to advertising: he illustrated numerous campaigns for various agencies. Grey, Euro RSCG Works, Renault, Perrier, Vittel, Heineken, Tabasco, Oxbow called on his services, along with the French AIDS Information Service: he produced a modern Snow White and a flirtatious Cinderella for a public-awareness campaign. Fluent in various styles and media, Boogaerts has devoted himself since 1997 to the creation of digital imagery for television companies, while continuing his involvement with advertising and the press. He recently produced the illus-

tration that accompanied the opening of Louis Vuitton stores in New York, as well as a series of drawings for *Montres Magazine*. Hermès and the magazine *Intramuros* are two of his newest clients. He is currently preparing the exhibition of a series of 16 drawings reproduced as screen prints, on the theme of the mythical and oft-revisited image of James Bond. It will begin its tour in September 2006. He is also working on the publication of a children's book about design icons.
Pages: 186, 187

## Frédéric BORTOLOTTI

Frédéric Bortolotti is an artist and illustrator but, above all, a graphic designer. After training in applied arts at the Olivier de Serres school, he started out working with the designer Alain Carré, then entered Alain Lachartre's team at Vue sur la Ville before joining that of Bernard Baissait. In 1993, he founded the review *Bulldozer*, midway between a collector's catalogue and art review, which would run until 2003. He met Pascal Béjean, with whom he founded Labomatic in 1997; they were then joined by P. Nicolas Ledoux and Sylvie Astier. They were looking for a new approach to artistic production, preferring the term "collective" to that of studio. Throughout their work, Bortolotti and Béjean sought to establish a form of narration that played with the relationship between text and image and the frontiers between the disciplines. They acquired a loyal following by fomenting experimentation and reinterpreting major artistic trends. In 2000, Bortolotti founded Ultralab, a distinct but complementary entity, to promote the group's artworks. This was responsible, for example, for the visual publicity for the Théâtre des Amandiers in Nanterre, for which he used found photographs. Bortolotti has collaborated with the Musée d'Art Moderne de la Ville de Paris, La Villette and the AFAA (on the Flux project, 2001) and he regularly designs exhibition catalogues, CD covers and multimedia projects.
Pages: 177, 190

## Steven BURKE

Born in Germany in 1982, Burke first developed his artistic talents with the graffiti that he created in parallel to his studies at the School of Visual Communication in Bordeaux. After working for several public relations agencies and serving an apprentice-

ship in New York with the Japanese artist Takashi Murakami in 2003, Burke began a regular collaboration with the Parisian design agency SublimDesign. His influences run from Chris Ware to Cinderella. His illustrations are mainly portraits: children, dynamic thirtysomethings, computer hackers… His style, with its thick outline, is close to that of mangas and independent comics. Since 2004, his illustrations have appeared in magazines such as *Wad*, *Studio*, *Têtu*, *Happens* and *Stratégies*. He lives and works in Bordeaux, where he exhibited his work in 2006.
Page: 82

## Max CABANES

The French comic scripter, artist and illustrator Max Cabanes was born in 1947 in Béziers. Self-taught, he developed a comic called *Démons et Merveilles*, and this led to work for the magazines *Paris Match* and *Record* in 1971. Four years later, he created the review *Tousse Bourrin* – which lasted for four issues – and he joined the magazine *Fluide glacial* in 1977. From then on he contributed to *Pilote*, *À suivre*, *Charlie*, *L'Humanité* and took part in several group books, including *Paris sera toujours Paris(?)* (Dargaud, 1981) and *Contes fripons* (Audie, 1982). It was *Dans les villages*, his first comic book (1976), which revealed his pure, precise line and his talent as a narrator. The action takes place in the South of France – a landscape that recurs in his work – in an atmosphere typical of the 1960s. The confessional *Colin-Maillard*, published in 1989, marked a nostalgic turn; he plunged back into childhood, in a dreamlike spirit tinged with humour but also with angst. In *Rencontres du troisième sale type* (Les Humanoïdes Associés, 1991) and *Les Années pattes d'eph'* (Albin Michel, 1992), his style finally erupted. Many books were to follow, including *Bellagamba*, with a script by Patrick Cauvin, alias Klotz (Casterman), and *Bouquet de flirts*, which he produced with Sylvie Brasquet (Albin Michel). In 1996 he was awarded the Grand Prix de la Ville and the Specialised Libraries prize at the Angoulême International Comics Festival. Max Cabanes has also illustrated numerous works for the publishers Syros, Mango Jeunesse, Dargaud and L'École des Loisirs. His latest book is called *L'École de la cruauté* (Dupuis, 2005).
Pages: 45, 130

## Cyril CABRY

Cyril Cabry was born in 1967 in Oran, Algeria. He attended the École Estienne before starting out as an art director in the print media. In 1989, he produced his first book, *El Rebelde, le rebelle*, on a scenario by François Avril (Futuropolis, 1989). At the same time, he was providing illustrations for various magazines in France and the United States: *The New Yorker*, *The Boston Globe*, *Globe*, *Max*, *Biba*, *Madame Figaro*, *The New York Times*, *Enjeux les Échos* and *Maison Française*. In the field of illustration, his versatility has led him to collaborate with such diverse publishers as Running Press, Futuropolis, Albin Michel and Nathan, with whom he published *Le Vélo, c'est trop dur!* and *Mimi La Montagne*. He also directs the creative side of a Parisian public relations agency. In 2005, he founded BY, a brand which he co-runs with his partner Mely: together, they invent and produce motifs to be used on various supports – T-shirts, bags, cushions, etc. He belongs to the association Le Crayon.
Pages: 56, 57, 74

## CARLOTTA

Born in Lyon in 1959, Carlotta first of all studied at the Beaux-Arts then at Studio Berçot in Paris, where she studied design before becoming assistant to the director, Marie Rucki. Soon she was working for fashion magazines all over the world, and her elegant, quintessentially Parisian women were appearing in many guises both in the press and on the screen. Her long-legged, skinny models have huge eyes; they look like liberated reflections of a spirited French fashion designed in their image. They have been published in magazines like *Vogue*, *Marie-Claire*, *Libération*, different international editions of the magazine *Elle* – for which she also designed the Internet site – and even *Spur*. She has illustrated many advertising campaigns: Azzaro, Kookaï, Sveltesse (her characters can be seen in animation on the website of Azzaro perfume company); she has worked with Dim, for whom she designed packaging, and the brands L'Oréal and Intimate, for whom she created logos. She has also worked for television, producing the graphic landscape for the programme *Film du jour* (Paris Première). Carlotta's candy-pink world can be seen on all kinds of supports: fashion objects, textiles, etc. She has decorated the store windows of Kookaï and Printemps in Paris. Carlotta

was one of the illustrators chosen for the exhibition *Traits très mode* at the Bon Marché in March 2005. She is one of the emblematic figures of French fashion illustration and so her work is regularly included in books on the subject. *Carlotta, autoportraits de A à Z*, her guide to the trendy Parisian woman, has been exclusively published in Japan.
Pages: 59, 63, 82, 194, 223, 224

## Philippe CARON

Born in Normandy in 1944, Philippe Caron studied book art and design at the Ecole Estienne before joining Snip, Jacques de Pindray's agency. His departure for New York with Antoine Kieffer, the artistic director of *Marie-Claire*, marked an important turning point in his career. His first comics were published in 1964. He subsequently worked for *The New Yorker*, *Lui*, *Lire*, *Vogue Germany* and *Madame Figaro* while illustrating several children's books, including *La Teryel et le Cheval rouge, conte berbère* in 1986 and *Rama et le Prince bleu, légende indienne* in 1989 (Hatier). His command of a variety of styles led him to work on advertising campaigns for IBM, Louis Vuitton, L'Oréal and Crédit Agricole among others, and to design theatre sets. In recent years, he has co-written and illustrated *Drôles d'aventures, parfum volé* in 1998, and illustrated *Le Mystère Éléonor* by Évelyne Brisou-Pellen in 1999, which plunged the reader into 18th-century Brittany (Folio Junior). More recently, he published *Les Douze Travaux d'Hercule* with Christian Grenier (Nathan, 1999). Philippe Caron teaches drawing at the National School of Decorative Arts in Paris.
Pages: 27, 29, 32

## Yves CHALAND

The creator of Jeune Albert, Freddy Lombard, Bob Fish and Adolphus Claar died in 1990 at the age of 33. This exceptional artist, born in 1957, reinterpreted the comic book in the 1980s along with Serge Clerc, Ted Benoit and Floc'h. By the age of 17, he had already had work published in the fanzine *Biblipop*, before going on to study fine arts at Saint-Étienne; in 1976, he launched a fanzine with Luc Cornillon, *L'Unité de valeur*. Spotted by Jean-Pierre Dionnet, the editor of *Métal hurlant*, he joined the magazine as a designer and also published his first cartoons there. His chameleonic

style with borrowings from the 1950s, his nods to the Belgian masters Jijé, Tillieux, Franquin, his lucidity, unbridled humour and detailed landscapes are much appreciated by connoisseurs. He was taken up by magazines such as *Télérama*, *Reader's Digest* and *Best*. With Luc Cornillon, he published *Captivant* (Les Humanoïdes Associés, 1979), an anthology in which he explored a wide range of styles. In 1982, the *Aventures du Jeune Albert* appeared for the first time. Yves Chaland divided his time between his own work and advertising commissions worthy of his impeccable style. In Belgium, he published *Le Testament de Godefroid de Bouillon* in 1981 and *Adolphus Claar* in 1983 (Magic-Strip). Having always been attracted by Spirou's characters, Spit and Fantasio, Yves Chaland was going to continue their adventures. Some tentative experiments bear witness to this desire, but, finally, it was not to be; the strips that were completed, *Cœurs d'acier*, appeared in the book *Fantasio et le Fantôme* (Dupuis, 2003). While developing the character of Jeune Albert in *Métal hurlant*, Yves Chaland published the most interesting of his stories with Humanoïdes Associés: *Le Cimetière des éléphants* (1984), *La Comète de Carthage* (1986, scripted by Yann), *Vacances à Budapest* (1988, scripted by Yann) and *F.52* (1989, scripted by Yann). His last book, *La Main coupée*, with Jean-Luc Fromental, was published in 1990 by Nathan. At least two books have been devoted to him: *Chaland*, in 1995, and *Chaland et les Publicitaires*, in 2000 (Champaka Book, Brussels).
Pages: 190, 210, 226, 228

## Pierre CLÉMENT

Born in 1948 in Paris, Pierre Clément studied architecture at the Beaux-Arts and graduated in 1972. His heart, however, was in illustration. For two years, he created animal comics for the magazine *Téléparade* and monthly splash-page illustrations with no dialogue in *Métal hurlant*, on the theme of: "the forbidden"; in 1988 they were collected in an book entitled *Ralentir passage d'animaux* (Futuropolis), which was then adapted for television. He received the Grand Prix de Parigraph. As a scripter and artist, with his continuous and regular line born of his art-school studies, Pierre Clément has constructed a world made of all kinds of animal species "organised intel-

ligently in a well-structured world". He also illustrates for advertising and public relations and has worked on several campaigns, for clients such as Renault and Galeries Lafayette. In 1985, he produced several animations for Reynolds pens. The early 1990s were given over to books, with the publication of *Tralalajahal*, a book and portfolio of screen prints (Éditions Reporter, 1991), followed by three books from the series *Les Souris*, in 1992 and 1993 (Méphistopoulos). He also illustrated work in *The New Yorker* and produced a short animated film, *Silenzio & Tralala*, for Canal + in 1995. His animal world has inspired various decorative and ornamental creations in mosaic, stained glass, wrought iron, etc. He lives and works in Paris.
Pages: 175, 182, 184, 185, 190, 226, 228, 231, 234, 239, 241

## Serge CLERC

The author, comic artist and illustrator Serge Clerc, born in Roanne in 1957, was a figurehead for *Métal hurlant*: he published his first comics there in 1975, at the age of 18, and continued doing so until the magazine ended in 1987. He elegantly combines his love of the Clear Line, Art-Deco graphics and 80s' rock iconography. He has designed several record covers for artists such as Carmel and Joe Jackson, has contributed to the magazines *Rock & Folk*, *Best*, the British *Melody Maker* and *New Musical Express* and the Japanese *Player*. He is the author of *La Légende du rock'n'roll* (Les Humanoïdes Associés, 1984). In 1981 Magic-Strip published *Sam Bronx et les Robots*, while Humanoïdes Associés published *Le Dessinateur espion!* in 1978, *Captain Futur* in 1979, *Rocker* in 1981, *Mémoires de l'espion* in 1982, *La Nuit du Mocambo* in 1983 and *Meurtre dans le phare* (with François Landon) in 1986. The 1990s were devoted to press illustration: *Libération*, *Le Figaroscope*, *Cosmopolitan* and the *Herald Tribune*. His two latest books, *Les Limaces rouges*, in 1999, and *L'Irrésistible Ascension*, in 2000 (Éditions Reporter), mix surrealism and humour in short stories. His main illustrations have been collected in *Artiste et Modèle* (Albin Michel, 1987). In late 2006, he published, under the supervision of Jean-Luc Fromental at Denoël Graphic, *Métal hurlant story*, the tale of the legendary magazine told and illustrated today, in the style of the era, by those who took part in its adventure. Serge

Clerc lives and works in Paris. He is a member of the association Le Crayon.
Pages: 176, 190, 212, 226, 228, 229, 231, 233, 239, 241

## Paul COX

Born in 1959 in Paris, Paul Cox is an author, illustrator, painter, graphic designer and sculptor who crosses many worlds with a style and talent distinctly his own. He studied history of art and also English, which he taught before devoting himself to painting and children's publishing. *The Adventures of Archibald the Koala*, which have been adapted for television and broadcast in Europe and in Japan, have assured him international recognition. As a creator of playful images, Paul Cox loves experimentation and poetry. He has retained a child-like innocence while building abstract worlds using simple forms and juggling with construction, repetition and his own unique vocabulary. Over the course of his career, he has produced some fifteen books, including, for Seuil Jeunesse, *Histoire de l'art*, prize winner at the Salon de Bologne in 1999, *Ces nains portent quoi?* (2001), *Cependant* (2002) and *CoxCodex 1* (2003), which gathered together all his work since 1988, and *Mon Amour* (2005). Paul Cox also provides illustration for the press: *Family*, *Libération*, *Le Monde*, *Télérama* and *Lire*. He has designed posters for the Nancy Opera since 1996, as well as creating logos for Seuil Jeunesse and Albin Michel, among others. He has designed numerous CD covers for the Belles Lettres collection. Another facet of his talent is his advertising illustrations for the *Libération* newspaper and the Paris City Council. He has directed a series of advertising animations for Cegetel. He divides his time between Paris and his studio in Burgundy.
Page: 105

## Jean-Philippe DELHOMME

Born in 1959, Jean-Philippe Delhomme studied animation at the National School of Decorative Arts in Paris: he graduated in 1985. His early comics were published from 1983 in France. In 1987, *Glamour* published a series, *Polaroids de jeunes filles*. The compilation of these in book form (Albin Michel, 1989) established his reputation. Jean-Philippe Delhomme writes all his own texts, handling words like images. He is also the author of several novels published by Denoël, includ-

ing *Mémoires d'un pitbull* (1999) and *La Dilution de l'artiste* (2001). He is nevertheless best known for his work as an illustrator. He takes a critical look at his navel-gazing contemporaries, the world of fashion, art galleries, literary figures and comedians. In *Le Drame de la déco* (Denoël, 2000) and above all *Art Contemporain* (Denoël, 2002), he captures spitting images of artists, gallery owners and collectors. He manipulates ink like a scalpel, rarely with spite, but always with caustic humour. Each illustration is captioned with flashes of wit, complementing his fluid lines and attention to detail. In the 1990s, he went to show his work in New York and met the creative bosses of Barney's New York. This encounter gave rise to a series of campaigns that broke with the usual use of photography in the domain of fashion and took the form of press advertisements, billboards and animated films. Over the following years, he developed his work as an animator, producing seven commercials for Saab aimed at the American market. At the same time, he worked for *Vogue*, *House & Garden*, *The New Yorker* and *Town & Country*, and in 2000 he published a children's book, *Visit to Another Planet*. He has also illustrated posters for films like Pedro Almodóvar's *Tie me Up! Tie me Down!* and, more recently, *Darwin's Nightmare*. In 2006, he designed a poster campaign for Le Bon Marché. After *La Chose littéraire*, a collection of comics published in 2002 by Denoël in which he parodied the vanities of the literary world, he brought out a novel, *Comique de proximité* (Denoël, 2005): this time he turned his attention to comedians who have turned into media icons. His work appears regularly in *GQ* (United States) and *A.D.* (France).
Pages: 190, 214-218

## Isabelle DERVAUX

Born in Valenciennes in 1961, Isabelle Dervaux is a self-taught illustrator who graduated in history of art from the university of Lille. She is passionate about New York, and is in fact married to a New-Yorker (although she now lives San Francisco). She has worked with several publishers – principally Random House and Harper Collins. Her most notable work includes illustrations for *Melanie Jane*, *The Sky is Always in the Sky* and *Girls Club Kit*. She has been published in the international press, including *The New Yorker*, *The New*

York Times, Newsweek, Rolling Stone, etc. Playful, mischievous and childlike are the adjectives that spring to mind to describe her work. She has worked on several advertising campaigns for WH Smith London, McDonald's, Barney's New York, Tic Tac… And she has won numerous prizes. Some of her illustrations form part of the permanent collection at New York's MOMA.
Pages: 72, 73, 190

### Jean-Yves DUHOO

Born in 1965 in Lyon, Jean-Yves Duhoo studied at the National School of Applied Arts in Paris. He started out as a designer then published his first comics in the mid-1980s in the fanzines *Lapin*, *Fusée* and *Ego comme X*. He proved his versatility by going on to oversee the production of books for the publisher L'Association, an experience that he recounted in *Sainte Fabrique*, published in 2002. He has worked with *Libération*, illustrating the "Tentations" column. His work can also be seen in *Science et Vie Junior* and *Capsule cosmique*. A traveller with a finger in every pie, Jean-Yves Duhoo has even taught drawing in Japan. He won acclaim for educational projects such as *Électricité: qu'y a-t-il derrière la prise?* (an exhibition at the Cité des enfants at La Villette) and *Écoloville*, published by Hachette, a work taking a humorous look at man, nature and the nature of man. With his latest book, *L'Inconnu à la déverse* (Lito, 2006), scripted by Dorothée de Monfreid, Jean-Yves Duhoo this time takes us on a trip into the world of juvenile delinquency, with captivating results.
Pages: 66, 76

### DUPUY & BERBÉRIAN

The components of this Parisian duo specialising in comic books, illustration and graphic art are well nigh inseparable. Philippe Dupuy was born in Sainte-Adresse in 1960 and studied at the School of Decorative Arts in Paris. Charles Berbérian was born in Bagdad, Iraq, in 1959, and studied at the Beaux-Arts in Paris. The two artists met in 1982, at the fanzine *PLG*, then worked together on *Band'à part*, co-signing their scripting and artwork.
The latter was collected for the first time in *Les Héros ne meurent jamais* (L'Association, 1991). It was through Gotlib, in 1984, that they began working for the magazine *Fluide glacial*, which gave birth to Red, Basile and

Gégé, characters collected in the books *Graine de voyous* (Fluide glacial, 1987) and, above all, *Le Journal d'Henriette* (Les Humanoïdes Associés), the chronicle of a hung-up teenager, a series that began in 1988 and has carried on until today. They draw their stories with a perfect line, in total symbiosis, and with a perfect command of colours – it is impossible to spot which of the two does what. Humour is also coupled with seriousness and their characters are ironic or solitary dandies, like *Monsieur Jean* (Les Humanoïdes Associés), a Parisian writer portrayed in a series of books that began in the 1990s. They received the prize for the best comic book at the Angoulême International Comics Festival in 1999 for *Monsieur Jean, Vivons heureux sans en avoir l'air* (volume IV). In 1994, they produced one of their masterworks: the *Journal d'un album* (L'Association, 1994) then, between 1996 and 2004, they delivered their vision of New York, Barcelona, Tangier and Lisbon in the form of travel notebooks published by Cornélius. Apart from this, Dupuy & Berbérian have worked together on advertisements for the Nicolas wine shops, as well as for Chantal Thomass, Bonux and the SNCF. They have designed film posters for: *Au nom d'Anna* (2000), *The Navigators* (2002), *Mondovino* (2004)… Their work appears regularly in *Télérama*, *Libération*, *Le Nouvel Observateur*, *Dépêche Mode*, *Le Figaro*, *Les Inrockuptibles*, *Géo*, *Cosmopolitan*, *The New Yorker* and *The Washington Post*. On their own, Philippe Dupuy has published *Hanté* (Cornélius, 2005) and Charles Berbérian *Playlist* (Naïve, 2004). Their latest joint venture, *Un certain équilibre*, the seventh volume of *Monsieur Jean*, was published in 2005 by Dupuis. The work of these figureheads of the new wave of comic-book art has been seen all over the world.
Pages: 74, 112, 113

### FLOC'H

Jean-Claude Floc'h, known simply as Floc'h, was born in 1953. His father and uncle worked as printers, and this perhaps explains his relish for paper and love of books. He studied at the Paris School of Decorative Arts in the early 1970s. In 1977, he published his first comic in *Pilote*, *Le Rendez-vous de Sevenoaks*, with François Rivière – like him, a literature buff keen on English references, but also the

successor to Edgar P. Jacobs. Several books followed: *Le Dossier Harding* (1980), *Blitz* (1983), *À la recherche de sir Malcolm* (1984). Meanwhile, he exploited his talent in advertising and press illustration by contributing to magazines such as *The New Yorker*, *Lire*, *Monsieur*…
Inventing, creating worlds, hijacking reality: this is what he did in two little leaflets, *Life* and *High Life* (Carton, 1985 and 1986), delicious anthologies of fake covers of the famous magazine *Life*, where he paid homage to favourite artists, writers and painters. He has published *Jamais deux sans trois* (Albin Michel, 1991), *Ma Vie* (Les Humanoïdes Associés, 1985; Dargaud, 1994) with Jean-Luc Fromental; *Journal d'un New-Yorkais* (Dargaud-Champaka, 1994, with Michel Jourde) and *Meurtre en miniature* (Dargaud, 1994, with François Rivière). He created several film posters, for works such as *Smoking-No Smoking* by Alain Resnais (1993) and Woody Allen's *Deconstructing Harry* (1994) and *Hollywood Ending* (2002). Since the 1990s he has devoted himself to painting and regularly exhibits in Paris. His foremost illustrations have been collected in the books *Un homme dans la foule* (Albin Michel, 1985) and *Floc'h illustrateur* (Champaka, 2005). In 2005, he made a remarkable return to comic books with François Rivière when they invented the "first biography of a comic-book heroine", *Olivia Sturgess 1914-2004* (Dargaud).
Pages: 2, 31, 87, 116, 117, 183, 190, 191, 200, 201, 208, 209, 226, 227, 229, 231, 234, 239, 240

### Éric GIRIAT

Born in Paris in 1967, Éric Giriat studied at the Met de Penninghen studio then at the National School of Graphic Art, where he was particularly interested in the collage techniques taught by Roman Cieslewicz. He graduated in 1989 and started out publishing artwork in the magazine press: *7 à Paris*, *Lui*, *Cosmopolitan* or *Libération*. Extremely versatile, he likes to vary his subjects and detests being pigeonholed. He is passionate about fashion, economics and literature, while maintaining his taste for poetic collages. His style has evolved and he has mixed techniques – not only the inevitable collage but also gouache and pencil. He was discovered by *Première* in 1995 and, above all, by *Elle*, with whom he began a collaboration in 1996 that was virtually weekly

– and is still continuing today. His work can be seen in *Le Nouvel Économiste*, *Le Monde*, *Les Échos*, and *Phosphore* in France; *Focus*, *Brigitte* and *Eltern* in Germany, and *Better Homes & Gardens* and *The Economist* in the United States. His illustrations regularly appear in *Elle International*, which has brought him fame in Asia, Japan and Russia. He illustrates covers for various publishing houses, such as Robert Laffont, Albin Michel, Pocket and J'ai Lu. He has worked on advertising campaigns: Banque Populaire, Wanadoo, France Télécom, L'Oréal, Yahoo and, in the United States, Celltech and United Airlines in 2005. Éric Giriat has also dipped his toes into the world of fashion, working for Dominique Lila, Ralph Kemp and the German brand Joop!
Pages: 86, 146

### GOTLIB

Gotlib was born, under his real name of Marcel Gotlieb, in Paris in 1934. The son of Romanian Jews, he escaped from the Gestapo in 1942. After World War II, he became an accountant, while also studying at the National School of Applied Arts. He made his publishing debut in 1962 in the *Vaillant* magazine (now *Pif Gadget*), where he dreamt up various characters – Gilou, Klop, Puck and Poil, Nanar and Jujube. While working for *Record* magazine, he invented Professor Frédéric Rosbif, who would later become the celebrated Professor Burp. In 1965, he created, in collaboration with René Goscinny, the *Dingodossiers*, published in *Pilote*, then, in 1968, he thought up the *Rubrique-à-brac*. In 1971, he created the irresponsible chief scout *Hamster Jovial* in *Rock & Folk*. In 1972, he founded *L'Écho des Savanes* with Claire Bretécher and Nikita Mandryka. That same year, he appeared in *L'An 01*, Jacques Doillon's film based on the work of Gébé, in which he played the role of a prison warden. On the 1st of April, 1975, he founded the now legendary *Fluide glacial* with Jacques Diament, a magazine dedicated to "humour and the comic". The following year, he co-wrote the Patrice Leconte film *Les Vécés étaient fermés de l'intérieur*. He has acted in several films, but has never given up drawing and has created more characters – Gai-Luron, Pervers Pépère, Rhââ Lovely and Superdupont being the best known. In 1991, he won the main prize at the Angoulême International Comics Festival and an exhibition, *EuroGotlib-*

*Land*, was devoted to him the following year. His capacity to be both serious and funny was evident in *J'existe, je me suis rencontré* (Flammarion, 1993), an autobiographical novel in which he recounted his childhood under the Occupation. He would go on to direct an animated series about culture for Canal +, which gave birth to *Rubrique-à-brac Gallery*. His latest album, *Inédits*, published by Dargaud in 2006, is a collection of strips that could have figured in the *Rubrique-à-brac* or the *Dingodossiers*. To compile it, he gathered together illustrations that appeared in *Pilote*, *L'Écho des Savanes*, *Rock & Folk*, *Fluide glacial*, *Actuel* and *Hara-Kir*, between 1965 and 1980.
Page: 108

### Jean-Claude GÖTTING

Jean-Claude Götting, who was born in 1963, is an illustrator, graphic designer, scripter and painter. He trained at the Duperré School of Applied Arts, while also taking his first steps in the world of the comic with the fanzine *PLG*. In 1986, while still a student, he received the prize for the best first comic book at the Angoulême International Comics Festival with *Crève-Cœur* (Futuropolis, 1985). Several titles were to follow, always with Éditions Futuropolis: *Détours* (1986), *La Serviette noire* (1986), *La Fille du modèle* (1988), *Le Chemin des Trois Places* (1989) – with François Avril – and *L'Option Stravinsky* (1990). His world is intimate, depicted in black and white with his own distinctive technique: a thick outline, often combined with a viewpoint from a slightly low angle. His narratives are tinged with melancholy. As well as drawing, Götting creates stories for his colleagues. He is not always faithful to comic books, however, as he regularly moonlights with the press. We can find him, in colour this time, using acrylic paint for illustrations in magazines such as *Elle*, *Lire*, *Le Point*, *Courrier International*, *Phosphore*, *Jazzman* and *The New Yorker*. He has collaborated with several publishers, including Actes Sud, Denoël, Bayard, Nathan, Hachette, Futuropolis and Gallimard. Jean-Claude Götting became widely known to the general public, however, through his illustrations for the covers of the French edition of the various volumes of the *Harry Potter* saga. He has been responsible for many posters, including that of the musical comedy *Oliver Twist* in 2002. In the advertising field, he has worked with

BMW, Leffe and Cegetel. The year 2004 marked his big comeback to comics: *La Malle Sanderson*, an album published by Delcourt, was nominated for prizes at festivals in Angoulême, Tours and Monaco. He also received the City of Geneva's international award in 2004. His paintings are regularly exhibited in Paris.
Pages: 29, 43, 74, 75, 99, 190

## IZAK

Born on the outskirts of Paris, Izak studied at the Applied Arts School with a view to becoming a fashion designer. He began a regular collaboration with trend forecasters such as Carlin International and Promostyl. In 1992, he turned towards illustration and started producing figures that were feminine, gracious, slender and elegant – in short, very Parisian. These figures evolved as they appeared in magazines like *Dépêche Mode*, *Madame Figaro*, *Marie-Claire*, *Mademoiselle*, *Elle*, *Vogue*, *The New Yorker* and *The New York Times Magazine*. These reflections of fashions and trends also made appearances in advertising campaigns: Paul Smith, Chanel, Franck & fils, Bally, Monoprix, Le Printemps – for whom he also works in Tokyo – and the Spick and Span chain of stores – a campaign that won him a Merit Award from the New York Club of Art Directors. Since 1998, he has divided his time between Tokyo, New York – his home base – and Paris. He has produced children's books while simultaneously pursuing his work with luxury brands like Céline, for whom he designed a series of scarves, the Henri Bendel department store in New York and the Neiman Marcus chain.
Pages: 51-55, 126, 127, 132, 133

## Benoît JACQUES

Born in Brussels in 1958, Benoît Jacques studied in the city's Royal Academy of Fine Art and then at the National School of Visual Arts in La Cambre. It was in London, however, that he began illustrating and started to get known. He stayed there for ten years. He collaborated with the Pentagram agency, a temple of graphic design, which allowed him to discover all the possibilities of graphics. Returning to France in 1991, he relaunched the trend for the *flip book*, publishing little books himself when publishers refused to touch his projects. He learnt all the stages of book production, from the scenario to the manufacturing. In these Lilliputian

books, he reinvented the world, which he recounted with a childlike viewpoint and style, mixing poetry and humour. The success was immediate: since *Play it by ear* in 1989, more than thirty books have been produced, including *Le Jardin du trait* (1995). At the same time, he has illustrated or published books such as *Elle est ronde* (1997) and *Sagesses et Malices des dieux grecs* (2004) with Albin Michel Jeunesse, *La Fête des pères* (1992) and *Louisa* (2001) with L'École des Loisirs and *Salto solo* (L'Inventaire, 2001) and *Comique Trip* (Benoît Jacques Books, 2001). He regularly works for the French press, including *Le Monde*, *Télérama*, *Libération* and *Le Magazine littéraire*. Among his most recent titles are, from Benoît Jacques Books, *Je te tiens* (2003), *Chat!* (2004), *Attention extraterrestres* (2005) and, in 2006, *Bestiaire corse*, which he produced with Laurent Grisel.
He also paints and engraves. Benoît Jacques lives in the country, an hour away from Paris.
Pages: 138, 139, 179

## Martin JARRIE

Born in 1953 in La Verrie in the Vendée, Martin Jarrie – real name Jean-Pierre Moreau – is undeniably one of France's most appealing painters and illustrators, thanks to his style and the warmth of his subtly chosen colours. After a childhood spent reading *Le Petit Larousse illustré*, followed by studies at Angers School of Fine Art and a career as a commercial artist – hence the hyperrealism of his style – he changed track completely in his professional life by adopting the pseudonym Martin Jarrie, in homage to a farm in his village, and totally changed his graphic style. His vocabulary became phantasmagorical, drawing on childhood and dreams, and he turned towards press illustration, publishing and also advertising. His reinterpretation of history and art, his fauna – somewhere between real and imaginary –, his vegetables drawn on backgrounds of saturated ochre colours and his inverted perspectives delighted magazines like *Phosphore*, *Enjeux les Échos*, *Libération*, *Télérama* and *The New Yorker*. He created a floating universe, a world at once disquieting and familiar, peopled with characters with pointed noses, round bodies, long arms and off-the-wall hairdos. His first comic book, published in 1995 by Nathan, was *Toc, toc! Monsieur Cric-Crac!* (1995); *Le Colosse machi-*

*nal* followed in 1996. They were both prize-winners at the Bratislava Biennale in 1997. He has gone on to produce dozens of illustrated books and comic books, including *Princesse Anna* (1998) published yet again by Nathan, *Un petit air de famille* (Rue du Monde, 1998), *Les Étonnants Animaux que le fils de Noé a sauvés* (Rue du Monde, 2001), *Au bout du compte* (Éditions du Rouergue, 2002) and *Ceci est un livre* (Thierry Magnier, 2002). His "portraits" of fruits and vegetables for *Une cuisine grande comme un jardin* by Alain Serres (Rue du Monde, 2004) seemed to ripen on the page. In 2005, he illustrated *Bout de bois, d'après l'infatigable, l'inoxydable Pinocchio* by Jean Cagnard (Éditions du Bonhomme Vert).
Pages: 97, 98, 109

## Jean-Charles KRAEHN

This Breton scripter and artist, born in Saint-Malo in 1955, was trained in industrial graphics before he veered towards cartoons. He contributed to the review *Scouts de France* then worked for several children's book publishers, including Hachette, and illustrated history books and other titles for the Bibliothèque Verte. He became increasingly interested in comics and gave a fresh look at the depiction of history in *2 000 ans d'histoire de l'Oise*, an album commissioned by Crédit Agricole. He also participated in the collective book *2 000 ans d'histoire de la Bretagne*. In 1985, he published his first comic from the medieval series *Les Aigles décapitées*. 1990 saw the start of the series *Bout d'homme*, published by Glénat and, in 1993, Kraehn offered Éditions Dargaud the scenario for *Tramp*, a maritime saga drawn by Patrick Jusseaume. Three years later, he turned his attention to the contemporary detective novel with the police series *Gil Saint-André*, part of Glénat's "Bulle noire" collection. The series *Le Triangle secret* (Glénat), drawn by Didier Convard, was born in 1994. In his most recent comic books, *Le Ruistre* (Glénat, 2001) and *Myrkos*, illustrated by Miguel (Dargaud, 2004), Kraehn contributed to both the scripting and drawing. Along with Régis Loisel and Laurent Vicomte, he is one of the patrons of the Perros-Guirec Comics Festival.
Pages: 90, 91

## Anja KROENCKE

Anja Kroencke was born in Vienna (Austria) in 1968. After studying fashion

design at the Vienna College of Textile and Design and taking a course in graphic design, she became art director of the advertising agency GGK, one of the most important in Vienna. The turning point of her career, and her return to fashion illustration, occurred in 1994, in New York, where she had decided to settle, seduced by the energy of the city. She started drawing the long-limbed women with stylised and elegant figures that would become her trademark. Her illustrations combine gentleness and refinement. Anja Kroencke works with many of the big names in magazines: *Vogue*, *The New Yorker*, *Wallpaper\**, *The New York Times*, *Elle*, *Harper's Bazaar*, *Madame Figaro* and *Marie-Claire*. She has also worked for several major luxury brands – Shiseido, Givenchy, Estée Lauder, Tiffany Japan – as well as the Printemps department stores, Polygram and British Airways.
Pages: 62, 80, 83, 122, 123

## Valérie LANCASTER

Valérie Lancaster lives and works in Paris. After attending the National School of Decorative Arts, where she studied under Jean Widmer and Roman Cieslewicz, she collaborated with various agencies – Dorland & Grey, Publicis – then began a career as a freelance illustrator. Several magazines asked her to work for them: *Cosmopolitan*, *Elle*, *Biba*, *Marie-Claire*, *Votre Beauté*, *Vogue Hommes*... Her passion for fashion influences her style, which has brought her commissions from the international women's press: *Vogue* and *Madame Figaro* in Paris, *Vogue Japon* and *Figaro Japon* (for whom she produces the section "The Corridors of Fashion"), the Italian magazine *Grazia* (who made her sign an exclusive contract lasting several years to produce their main illustrations on the subject of cosmetics and perfumes) and *Glamour* in Germany. She has made several trips to Japan, where she was responsible for the image and form of the *Reciente* range of products from Shiseido. Guerlain, Chanel, Kenzo and Jill Sanders, among others, have all commissioned visuals from her. She has exhibited her work at the Ginza Art Space in Tokyo and at Marie Mercié's fashion house in Paris.
Page: 36

## Tinou LE JOLY SENOVILLE

Born in 1963 in Rennes, she studied

cinema and video at the National School of Decorative Arts in Paris. She began working beside Li Edelkoort and, as a freelance, took part in collaborations with other trend forecasters like Promostyl and Peclers. Meanwhile, she started to work for the press and in advertising, notably for *Marie-Claire*, *Le Figaro Madame*, *Le Figaro Décoration* – for two years running on the "Vu ailleurs" section –, *Libération* and *Jeune et Jolie*. Her woodcuts and highly poetic vision won great acclaim, and in the mid-1990s she started getting commissions from outside France, above all from the American press (*Harvard Business Review*, *The New Yorker*, *Chicago Tribune*…), publishers (Albin Michel in l'Hexagone, Running Press, Chronicle Books) and advertising. For the past three years, she has been developing her own brand of clothes and accessories for children, Petit Rétro, deeply inspired by illustration. She lives and works in Paris.
Pages: 1, 92, 93, 168, 169

## Pierre LE-TAN

Born in 1950 of a Franco-Vietnamese artist father and a Parisian mother, Pierre Le-Tan was one of the three first Frenchmen to have work published by the celebrated magazine *The New Yorker*, along with Sempé and André François. He had had the good idea of sending proposals for illustrations to a certain Jim Geraghty, whose name he had spotted on the pages of the magazine, to which his parents subscribed. He produced a cover in 1970, the first time his work had ever been published: he was just 19 years old. Some time later, he went to New York and met the man who had propelled him to the forefront of the scene. Twenty-five years of faithful and regular collaboration were to follow. Pierre Le-Tan acquired international fame, which led him to be published in the top international magazines and become a regular contributor to *Vogue* and *World of Interiors*. Though he was born in Paris, he remains marked by his Vietnamese origins and looks at the world with refinement and extreme elegance. He likes portraits and theatrical settings; he is concerned with architecture, style, fashion and atmosphere, creating a somewhat melancholic vision of the good life. His extremely narrative illustrations are like the beginnings of novels, or postcards sent from a Mediterranean town where time has stopped. With Aubier, he published

*Rencontres d'une vie* (1986) and *Album* (1990), which present his world as an illustrator. In 1978, his meeting with the writer Patrick Modiano marked the beginning of a rich collaboration: together, they would publish *Memory Lane* (Hachette, 1981), *Poupée blonde* (P.O.L, 1983) and *Villes du sommeil* (Gallimard, 1993). Pierre Le-Tan would also illustrate many covers of the paperback editions of Modiano's book. He regularly collaborates with English-language publishers and, in France, works for Hachette, P.O.L and Aubier. Pierre Le-Tan has designed film posters, and his drawings decorated the *Quadrille*, directed by Valérie Lemercier. He regularly exhibits in Paris, New York and Munich.
Pages: 35, 38-41, 102, 115, 129, 156-159, 198, 199

## LOUSTAL

This great traveller was born in Neuilly-sur-Seine in 1956. He trained as an architect at the Beaux-Arts in Paris. He took his first steps in book publishing with *Une vespa, des lunettes noires, une palm beach, elles voudraient en plus que j'aie de la conversation* (Rudler, 1980) – which collected the comic art he had contributed to the magazine *Rock & Folk* – and *Clichés d'amour* in 1982 (Les Humanoïdes Associés, 1982), then he published a collection of illustrations, *Zenata Plage* (Magic-Strip, 1983). With Philippe Paringaux, he was responsible, under the auspices of Casterman, for *Cœurs de sable* in 1985 and, above all, *Barney et la note bleue* (1987), the book which sealed Loustal's reputation. He teamed up with Jérôme Charyn to produce *Les Frères Adamov* (1991) and *White Sonya* (2000), also published by Casterman. He loves to plunge his readers into forgotten jazz-era settings, beach scenes and voyages on the China Seas. He is a peerless colourist whose work is closer to Fauvist painting than traditional comic-book art. He has a reporter's knack for setting a scene, whether in a port, on a beach or in a desert. Loustal, who spends a large part of the year travelling around the world, regularly brings back sketches and souvenirs which he assembles in *Carnets de voyages* (Seuil). His travel images have been published by various companies as beautiful limited editions of signed screen prints. He is also a press illustrator who regularly receives commissions from *Libération*, *Le Monde*, *Senso*, *Télérama* and *The New Yorker*. He has created film post-

ers, notably for *Un monde sans pitié* and *Comme elle respire*. His most recent works are *La Nuit de l'alligator* (2005) and *Le Sang des voyous* (2006), both published by Casterman. In 1998, he received the Alph'art for the best scenario for *Kid Congo* (Casterman, 1997) at the Angoulême International Comics Festival. Loustal is a great painter of colour, of women, of exoticism. His paintings are highly coveted by collectors: he exhibits every year in Paris and has also had shows all round the world.
Pages: 32, 43, 44, 68-71, 98, 106, 111, 136, 137, 172, 173, 182, 192, 230, 231, 234, 239, 241

## Mïrka LUGOSI

Born in the heart of Dracula's Carpathians in 1958, Mïrka Lugosi is as well-known for her press illustrations as for her erotic performances and happenings. Her Louise Brooks-like persona is a mysterious double. She plays hide-and-seek without hiding: on the one hand, an illustrator who collaborates with the magazines *Aden*, *Lire*, *Libération*, *Marie-Claire*, *Le Magazine littéraire* and *Télérama*; on the other, an artist who reveals a sensual but phantasmagorical world, in which the often cruel games of certain women – including her – merge fantasy and reality: self-portraits, gouaches, drawings, Polaroids, paintings on photographic prints and even video art are her chosen media. In the realm of eroticism, she was also the model for the postcard series *Les Culottes*, *Dans un monde d'hommes* and *C'est le moment de se brûler délicieusement les doigts*, published between 1998 and 2000 by *Derrière la salle de bains*. Her images are regularly exhibited in Paris: at the Galerie Philippe Luigi in 1991, at Larmes d'Éros in 1996, at the Erotic Art Museum in 1997, at the Netherlands Institute… Muse for the photographer Gilles Berquet, coeditor of the review *Maniac* to which she regularly contributes, she is a prime mover in the world of French fetishism. She is less well known for her achievements as a graphic designer, such as her work with the TV channels La Sept and Arte in the 1990s.
Pages: 134, 135

## Clare MACKIE

It is impossible not to recognise the distinctive animals of Clare Mackie, the Scottish-born illustrator who is deeply inspired by the natural world – bees

with globular eyes, flies, frogs, alligators, seahorses, cows and little pigs… Her style is playful, spirited, her colours lively and her wordplay pervasive. After five years of study in Edinburgh, she moved to London and became involved in public relations for big brands such as Neiman Marcus, Harvey Nichols, Chanel, IBM, Trish McEvoy, Macallan and, in the press and media, *The New Yorker*, *Harpers and Queen* and the BBC. Above all else, however, Clare Mackie is a children's book illustrator who counts among her publications *First Comes Love* (Workman Publishing Company, 2001), *Michael Rosen's Book of Nonsense* (Hodder, 1998) and the series *Crazy Creatures* (Zero to Ten). In 2005, she created her own company for publishing greetings cards. She lives and works in London.
Pages: 152-155

## Daniel MAJA

Born in Paris in 1942, trained in engraving at the École Estienne, Daniel Maja is both an illustrator and a journalist. He also teaches drawing for the press at the École Émile Cohl in Lyon. Using pen, ink and pastels, he describes and draws an inviting animal world with tenderness and mischievousness. He has published dozens of books for young readers with various publishers – *Un pruneau dans la citrouille* (Seuil, 1993), *La Vie brève* (Octavo, 1994), *Animaux de toutes sortes* (Bilboquet, 2001), *Sur les traces des dieux grecs* (Gallimard Jeunesse, 2005) and *Il était une fois… il était une fin* (Rue du Monde, 2006). He has also been responsible for film posters and the backgrounds of animated cartoons, as well as publishing an essay, *Illustrateur jeunesse: comment créer des images sur les mots?* (Éditions du Sorbier, 2004). He works for magazines such as *Lire*, *Le Magazine littéraire*, *L'Expansion*, the Bayard Presse group and *The New Yorker*. Daniel Maja lives and works in Saint-Mandé, near Paris.
Page: 43

## Frank MARGERIN

Born in Paris in 1952, this comic book artist studied at the School of Applied Arts, and graduated in textile design in 1974. It was in 1976, through the intercession of Jean-Pierre Dionnet, that Frank Margerin published his first strips, *Simone et Léon*, in *Métal hurlant*. In 1982, he created *Albert et Mauricette* and *Skoup et Max Flash*, but he is best known as the creator of the celebrated

Lucien, born in 1979, the blundering, soft-hearted suburban rocker with a quiff and big nose. A rocker himself, he designed several record covers, including those of the group he formed with Denis Sire, Jean-Claude Denis, Dodo and Vuillemin (Dennis' Twist, which disbanded in 1990). The comic-book *Bananes métalliques* (Les Humanoïdes Associés, 1982) crowned his career by selling out its print run of 100,000 copies. In 1989, the publisher Les Humanoïdes Associés commissioned him to edit group comic books under the generic title *Frank Margerin présente…* The same year, he worked on an animated series, putting on screen the adventures of *Manu*, which were broadcast in 1990 then adapted as a comic, in collaboration with the artist Altheau. In 1992, at the 19th Angoulême Festival presided over by Gotlib, Frank Margerin received the Ville d'Angoulême prize. In 1993 he brought out *Lucien, le retour*, followed by *Lucien aux États-Unis* and *Lucien, Week-end motard* in 2000. *Lucien 25 piges* appeared in 2004 (Les Humanoïdes Associés). In 2002, he created, for the magazine *L'Écho des Savanes*, a new character, Momo, Lucien's younger brother, the proud owner of a Vespa. After *Momo le coursier* (2002) and *Momo roule toujours* (2003), the third volume, *Le Grand Saut*, was published in 2005 (Albin Michel).
Page: 111

## Jean-François MARTIN

Jean-François Martin was born in Paris in 1967. After studies at the National School of Applied Arts, he became a graphic designer for the Bayard publishing house. He then started a career as freelance illustrator in France, the USA and Canada. Over the past fifteen years he has illustrated various books for the youth market for Nathan, Gallimard, Actes Sud, Albin Michel, and Mango… He published, among others, *Parfum de sorcière* (Nathan, 1996), *Gare au carnage, Amédée Petitpotage!* (Nathan, 2002), *La Dentriste* (Thierry Magnier, 2006) and *En route pour la montagne magique* (Bayard Jeunesse 2004), which collected the Chronos Maternelle-CP prize in 2005. Of equal note are *Charlie Chaplin* (2002) and *Le Tardieu* (2003) published by Mango Jeunesse. In press illustration, his signature can be found in *Le Monde*, *Libération*, *National Post Business*, *Challenges*, *Le Monde de l'éducation* and *Dada*.

His style is austere, sophisticated and amusing, and he particularly likes to revisit the 1950s. He composes his illustrations using paper cut out of mail order catalogues, which he combines with touches of gouache as precise as an illuminated manuscript.
Pages: 170, 180, 181

## Lorenzo MATTOTTI

Born in Italy in 1954, the painter and illustrator Lorenzo Mattotti is a multi-talented artist who uses a variety of techniques and supports, but always in a style that is extremely recognisable. After architecture studies in Venice, he turned towards graphic design, comics and fashion illustration, which he wanted to revive. A member of the artists' collective Valvoline (which he joined in 1979), he was discovered in 1986 with the publication of *Feux* (Albin Michel); hailed as a major event in the world of comic books, it went on to win him many prizes. He did not renounce illustration, however, and collaborated regularly with the magazine *Vanity*, where he offered a fresh look at the great couturiers. In 1987 these drawings were brought together in *Pour Vanity* (Albin Michel). Since then, his characteristic interlaced couples, painted in acrylic, have appeared in *Cosmopolitan*, *Paris Match*, *Panorama*, *Corriere della Sera* and on the cover of *The New Yorker*, *Télérama*, *Le Monde* and *Le Nouvel Observateur*. His distinctive qualities – the dreaminess of his images, the strength of his composition, the playing with perspective and the power of his portraits – have attracted the attention of numerous brands, to whom he has lent his confident lines and flamboyant colours. The Paris City Council has commissioned a series of posters announcing large cultural events and, in 2002, he produced the poster for the Cannes Film Festival. Lorenzo Mattotti has worked with several publishers: *Le Signor Spartaco* (Les Humanoïdes Associés, 1983), *Labyrinthes* (1988) and *Doctor Nefasto* (1989) with Albin Michel, *Stigmates* (Seuil, 1998) and *Le Pavillon sous les dunes* (Vertige Graphic, 1992). He also devotes himself to children's books: *Pinocchio* (Albin Michel, 1990) and *Eugenio* (Seuil, 1993), rewarded in 1993 by the main prize at the Bratislava Festival and later animated for TV and film. Outstanding among his recent books are *Docteur Jekyll & Mister Hyde* (Casterman, 2002), *Le Bruit du givre* (Seuil, 2003) and

*Angkor* (Seuil, 2004). Some of his most beautiful work is collected in *Les Affiches de Mattotti,* published by Seuil in 2003. He lives and works in Paris.
**Pages: 89, 124, 125, 202, 225**

## Christophe MERLIN

This author and illustrator was born in 1966 in Neuilly-sur-Seine. After training in page layout and design, he turned to publishing and the press, collaborating with Éditions Bayard. Christophe Merlin, whose virtuoso style uses collages on gouache as well as other techniques, loves to invent characters: the racing-car driver (homage to the pedal car he had as a child), worldly girls or a solitary traveller. They are caricatured, expressive and always charming, despite being badly proportioned and craggy. He also revels in the world of children's books, travel, the colonial past and exoticism. He is both author and illustrator of several books, including *La Maternelle* (1999), *La Sorcière* (2000) and *La Fille de l'air* (2001) published by Albin Michel. This eternal traveller also sends back his numerous travel notebooks, such as *Saint-Louis du Sénégal* (Albin Michel, 2004), for which he has received many prizes. He is the illustrator of *Moi, Ferdinand, quand j'étais pirate* (Nathan, 2005) and a host of books for Milan and Syros. In 2005, he made his first venture into adult comics with Casterman; *La Goule,* a work of fantasy, produced in collaboration with Agathe de la Boulaye.
**Pages: 100, 101**

## Ever MEULEN

Eddy Vermeulen, alias Ever Meulen, was born in Kuurne, Belgium, in 1946. His drawing studies at Saint-Luc (Ghent and Brussels), after a period at Courtrai, led him, in 1970, to the Belgian weekly *Humo,* for which he has worked regularly. His drawings, in an impeccable, sober and highly geometrical style with continuous lines, in the tradition of the Belgian school of the 1930s and 1950s, have been published by several magazines internationally: *The New Yorker, De Standaard* and, above all, *Raw,* the American review created by Art Spiegelman, which brought him a Certificate of Design Excellence – one of his numerous prizes. He loves beautiful cars with pure lines but also modern architecture, cinema, Memphis rock'n'roll and art history. His illustrations can be seen in large format via numerous screen prints and portfolios: *Huiles sur papier* (Futuropolis, 1984) and *Publi-*

*folio* (Plaizier [Bruxelles], 1984). He has designed many posters for music festivals and theatre, as well as set designs for Flemish television, covers for books and magazines, record covers and even stamps for the Belgian and Dutch postal services. He has also lent his touch to advertising and is an illustration teacher at the Académie Saint-Luc de Gand. In 1987, *Feu vert* (Futuropolis) brought together his most important illustrations. His career and his work since 1998 are collected in *Verve* (Year 2 Edition, 2006). His work has been exhibited all over the world.
**Pages: 34, 111, 140, 141**

## Walter MINUS

Born in 1958 in Rome, Walter Minus is a graduate of the National School of Applied and Industrial Art in Paris. He regularly illustrates articles for the magazine press: *Avantages, Elle, Senso, Lire, Marie-Claire, Cosmopolitan* and, in the United States, *The New Yorker* and *The New York Magazine.* Walter Minus loves women, delicious and angelic dolls, red-lipped pin-ups with perfect, generous figures. As a comic-book artist, he depicts them full-face, in profile, in black lace, almost nude, without speech bubbles but with captions, as they have already surrendered to the reader – even though they might seem rather difficult to please. The style is precise, the black outline subtle and economical, at the crossroads between the Clear Line and Pop Art. In the magazine *Blab!,* published in Seattle by Fantagraphics, his style is slightly different, more surrealistic: here, he produces, year in, year out, surprising images in which he experiments with new techniques. This unusual magazine is mainly distributed in modern-art museums around the world. Walter Minus is very much in demand for cover illustrations, often receiving commissions for Denoël, Flammarion, Albin Michel, Hachette, Le Livre de poche Jeunesse and L'Express Éditions. Renault, Kodak, Air France, Coca-Cola, EDF, the Swiss bank Oyster Funds – to mention just a few brands – have entrusted him with their image in France or abroad. Since *Ciao Poupée,* his first book, published by Les Éditions Magic-Strip in Brussels in 1983, there have followed *Vicky et Pamela* (Carton, 1985), *De si jolies filles !* (Magic-Strip, 1985), *Petit Souper fin* (Librairie Nation, 1987), *Succès d'amour* (Comixland, 1988), *Ton cœur moqueur* (Futuropolis, 1988), *Jamais content!*

(Les Mal Élevés, 1999), *Les Pirates et les Cow-Boys,* scripted by his son Lancelot Lachartre (Le Neuvième Monde, 2001), and *Noire Séduction* (Le Neuvième Monde, 2004). His latest book, *Darling Chéri,* came out in the United States in 2006 (Blab Books). Every year he publishes *Minus Magazine,* in which, over the course of thirty pages, he keeps us up to date with the adventures of his best friends. He is also much appreciated by children, for whom he creates stories in the review *Je bouquine* (Bayard Presse). Meanwhile, he pursues a career as a painter: his canvases are regularly exhibited in Paris and prized by connoisseurs. He lives and works in Paris.
**Pages: 35, 48-51, 63-65, 108, 145, 147-149, 190, 226, 228, 232, 235, 237, 239, 243**

## Aurore de la MORINERIE

Born in 1962 in Saint-Lô, Aurore de la Morinerie studied fashion design at the Duperré School of Applied Arts before becoming known as a freelance illustrator. Essentially, she uses the technique of wash drawings, which she applies to the world of plants and animals, and also to fashion. Her illustrations have been published in numerous magazines and newspapers, including *Elle* and *Le Monde,* where she has sketched fashion shows. She has also worked for several brands, such as Agnès b., Hermès and the Accor group. In 2005, she illustrated *Le Voyage d'Ulysse* (Réunion des Musées Nationaux). Today, she devotes a large part of her time to working in Japan and the United States.
**Pages: 60, 61**

## Iris de MOÜY

Born in 1975, Iris de Moüy entered the National School of Graphic Arts in Paris before pursuing her studies at the Helsinki University of Art and Design. She met the Japanese fashion designer Shinichiro Arakawa, who appreciated her liberated style and exhibited her drawings in Paris and Tokyo. He asked her to illustrate a series of T-shirts and objects, and they worked together on the exhibition *Paper Show.* After gathering attention in 2000, she produced numerous illustrations for the Japanese magazine *Commons & Sense,* and then received commissions in Europe from *Elle, Les Inrockuptibles, Jalouse, Spoon, Composite, Libération, Muteen,* etc. Her mischievous, girlish vision, fresh style and handwritten text mixed with illustrations attracted luxury brands

– Hermès, Cacharel and, in Japan, Honda and the Beams stores. For Éditions Autrement Junior, she published *Ils s'aiment* (2004), *Le Bonheur selon Ninon* and *La Vérité selon Ninon* (2005), awarded the Youth Press Prize in 2006. Her illustrations of the works of the Countess of Ségur, *Les Malheurs de Sophie, Les Petites Filles modèles, Les Vacances* and *Le Général Dourakine,* were published by Hachette in 2006. Iris de Moüy lives in Paris.
**Pages: 77-79**

## Marie PERRON

Born in 1965, Marie Perron studied at the Olivier de Serres School of Applied Art in Paris. She started out as a designer for Kenzo and designed shoes for the brand Free Lance before approaching the press with her own ideas for columns. This led to illustrations for "Top snob" in the *Figaroscope,* then "J'me l'fais" and "Do-dont" in *Jalouse.* In France, she contributes to *Cosmopolitan, Libération, Jalouse* and *Madame Figaro,* in Germany to *Glamour,* and in Italy to *Marie-Claire,* in which she publishes her spruce post-pin-ups – crazy fashion victims. She also creates fashion accessories: T-shirts for the Japanese brand Coigirlmagic, beach sets sold at Colette, stickers at Printemps Design. In the world of public relations, she works with brands such as Nomad, Soco, Shiseido and Contrex. In 2005, Marie Perron took part in the exhibition *Traits très mode* at the Bon Marché. In terms of books, she has illustrated *Fonelle et ses amis,* by Sophie Fontanel (Nil éditions, 2001) and was co-author – again with Sophie Fontanel – of *Savoir vivre efficace et moderne* (Nil éditions, 2003).
**Pages: 84, 85**

## Philippe PETIT-ROULET

Born in Paris in 1953, the artist and scripter Philippe Petit-Roulet published his first comic strips in the magazine *Zinc* in 1973. An illustrator and layout artist for the reviews *La Gueule ouverte* and *Antirouille* from 1974 to 1979, he started to contribute to *L'Écho des Savanes,* then met the director and screenwriter Didier Martiny. Together, they created short comic stories for *Pilote, Fluide glacial, Charlie, Hara-Kiri* and *Le Citron hallucinogène.* It was during this time that the duo created the character of Bruce Predator. They have published several books: *Face aux embruns* (Les Humanoïdes Associés, 1984), *Macumba River* (Dargaud, 1985),

*Bruce Predator, le cœur et la boue* (Casterman, 1985), *Le Cirque Flop* (Carton, 1987), *Humpf et la Schmockomobile* (Circonflexe, 1991) and *L'Objet invisible* (Cornélius, 2000). Petit-Roulet's style is varied: his drawings can be playful and childlike or, on the contrary, peopled by sinister-looking faces. His range of expression is large. He also produces illustrations for the press: *Le Monde, Lui, Marie-France, Télérama, Lire, Cosmopolitan, Marie-Claire* and *The New Yorker.* In 1993, he became known to the general public through the international advertising campaign for the launch of the Twingo, Renault's latest car. His posters and animations were seen all over the world. His fame extends to Japon, where the department stores Niji No Machi have called on his services. In 2002 he published *Bottin mondain* (Cornélius).
**Pages: 4, 75, 201, 202**

## Emmanuel PIERRE

Born in 1958, Emmanuel Pierre spent his childhood in Madagascar. Apart from his use of bright colours, his inspiration is mainly found at the back of old libraries, in books of magic spells and arcane dictionaries. His humorous drawings, peopled with animals, clowns and historical characters, resemble engravings – in fact, he draws with a quill and Indian ink. He cuts up old books to enrich his illustrations with a multitude of small details, mixing collages and burlesque characters; he completes his images with vegetation, costumes from another era or architectural elements. Emmanuel Pierre also provides illustrations for the press: *Lire, Libération, Le Monde* and *Marie-Claire.* His world is full of charm and elegance. He is the author of children's books, including *Timothée dans l'arbre* (Seuil Jeunesse 2003) and *Les Vingt et Une nuits* (Gallimard, 2005). He regularly exhibits his drawings in galleries, both in Paris and further afield.
**Pages: 30, 37, 88**

## Michael ROBERTS

Born in Aylesbury, England, Michael Roberts studied graphic arts at Wycombe High School in 1968 before plunging into the underground scene of Carnaby Street and starting out as a critic on the *Sunday Times,* where he became fashion editor. He joined the magazine *Tatler* as art director, then went on to *Vogue,* before becoming Paris editor for *Vanity Fair.* He has

published his illustrations and photos in *The New Yorker*, *L'Uomo*, *Vogue*, *The Sunday Times*, *V Magazine*, *The Independant* and *Interview*. At one and the same time an artist, critic and player in the world of fashion, Roberts has produced complex collages of haughty New York divas, or tribal dancers, drawing his influences from the 1930s – Matisse, Braque, Fernand Léger – but also from Pop Art. He "sketches" his victims with a primitive touch. Tina Brown, fashion editor of *Vanity Fair* and the *New Yorker*, and the founder of *Talk*, said of him in 1997: "He is the Cocteau of fashion." As a photographer, designer, director, illustrator and editor, Michael Roberts juggles disciplines while keeping an eye on the Zeitgeist and what fashion journalists are saying, capturing a season's crazes and documenting the people who will be wearing them. He is the author of several children's books – *Alphabet de la jungle* (1999) and *Mumbo Jumbo* (2000), published by Gallimard, and *Snowman in Paradise* (Chronicle Books, 2004), but he is also known for his books on fashion, including *Grace: Thirty Years of Fashion at* Vogue (7L, 2002) and, more recently, *M.r., The Snippy World of New Yorker Fashion Artist Michael Roberts* (Steidl, 2005).
Pages: 219, 221

## Marguerite SAUVAGE

Born in 1977, Chloé, alias Marguerite Sauvage, studied semiology and sociology, did a DESS in hypermedia and at the same time took art courses at the Atelier des Beaux-Arts in Paris and the Atelier Pastel du Louvre. After a period as a game designer, she became an illustrator in 2001. She is noted for her work in fashion, with her sketches of frivolous, 70s-style fashion victims. Her images are modern and refined; they create a special atmosphere, full of *joie de vivre*. They can be seen regularly in the press: *Elle*, *Cosmopolitan* and *Le Figaro*. Marguerite Sauvage has produced a wide range of material for public relations – Bouygues Telecom, Citroën, Galeries Lafayette, S.T. Dupont, Apple, Yves Rocher, Mattel, etc. – and has illustrated *Alice in Wonderland*, published in a 150th anniversary edition by la Bibliothèque Verte. She has also directed animation for the brands Cofinoga, Galeries Lafayette, Paul et Joe and, more recently, for Panasonic's website.
Pages: 220, 222

## Charlie SCHLINGO

Jean-Charles Ninduab, alias Charlie Schlingo, was born in 1955 and died in 2005, at the age of 50. An artist, scripter and illustrator, he was a familiar and colourful figure in the world of comic books, a member of Professor Choron's *Hara-Kiri* gang. It was in *Charlie mensuel* and in *Hara-Kiri* that he created the characters of Désiré Gogueneau and Josette de Rechange. His work was subsequently published by *Pilote*, *Métal hurlant*, *Le Petit Psikopat illustré* and *Ferraille illustré*. In 1991, he participated in the publication of *Grodada*, a children's review aimed at children as bad-mannered as him! Comic books followed: *Havanies primesautières* (Artefact, 1979), *Désiré Gogueneau est un vilain* (Futuropolis, 1982), *Patron, une cuite s'il vous plaît* (Albin Michel, 1999) and *Onulf le cybernéticien* (Les Requins Marteaux, 2001). Another facet of his talent was expressed as leader of the rock group Les Silver d'Argent.
Page: 110

## Jacques TARDI

Born in Valencia in 1946, Jacques Tardi spent his early years in post-war Germany – his father was a professional soldier. Historical conflicts and class war would inspire almost all his work. He would pay homage to the privates of the First World War with virtuosity, as in *La Véritable Histoire du soldat inconnu* (Futuropolis, 1974), *Adieu Brindavoine* and *La Fleur au fusil* (Dargaud, 1974) and *C'était la guerre des tranchées* (Casterman, 1993).
After a period at Lyon School of Fine Art, which he entered at 16, and further studies at the National School of Decorative Arts in Paris, Tardi started out at the magazine *Pilote* which has published his cartoons since 1969. Three years later, his first complete story appeared, with a script by Pierre Christin: *Rumeurs sur le Rouergue*, subsequently published by Éditions Futuropolis (1976). He then published regularly with Casterman, where he started the series *Les Aventures extraordinaires d'Adèle Blanc-Sec*; the first volume, *Adèle et la Bête*, appeared in 1976. He worked on several other series at the same time: he created the characters of Polonius (1977), of Arthur Meme (with Forest), and drew Nestor Burma, Léo Malet's famous detective. The latter series – still published by Casterman – started with *Brouillard*

au pont de Tolbiac (1982); followed by *120 rue de la Gare* (1988), *Une gueule de bois en plomb* (1990), *Casse-Pipe à la Nation* (1996), and *M'as-tu vu en cadavre?* (2000). Also of note are *Jeux pour mourir* (Casterman, 1992) and *Rue des Rebuts* (Alain Beaulet, 1990). He fulfilled one of his dreams by illustrating several novels by Céline for the Éditions Futuropolis-Gallimard: *Voyage au bout de la nuit*, (1988), *Casse-Pipe* (1989) and *Mort à Crédit* in 1991. Tardi has collaborated with several writers, including Daniel Prévost (*Sodome et Virginie*, Denoël, 1996), Jean-Patrick Manchette (the *Griffu* series, Le Square, 1978) and Didier Daeninckx (*Le Der des Ders*, Casterman, 1997). Tardi joined forces in 2001 to launch the saga *Le Cri du Peuple*, plunging their readers into the world of the Paris Commune. Jacques Tardi has won numerous awards, particularly the Ville d'Angoulême prize in 1985. He designed the poster for Federico Fellini's film *E la nave va* (*And the Ship Sails On*) in 1983, as well as that of *Uranus* by Claude Berri (1990). His latest project is the comic book adaptation of *Monsieur Cauchemar* by Pierre Siniac, a serialised detective novel; its strips were previewed in *L'Étrangleur* in March 2006 (Casterman). This monthly, 15-page, large-format magazine in black and white conjures up the Paris of the early of the 1960s.
Pages: 3, 18, 21-26, 46, 47, 107, 111, 177, 190

## Philippe VUILLEMIN

An artist and scripter born in Marseille in 1958, Philippe Vuillemin published his first comic in 1977 in the magazines *Hara-Kiri*, *Charlie Mensuel* and, above all, *L'Écho des Savanes*, which really made his reputation. An agitator with a cruel sense of humour and a nervy drawing style, Vuillemin hits hard, unafraid of breaking taboos, even if it means facing violent criticism – as, for example, after the appearance of his book *Hitler = SS*, conceived in 1986 with Jean-Marie Gourio but banned from bookshops. His early strips were collected in *Saine Ardeur* (1980) and *Sueurs d'hommes* (1980), from Éditions du Fromage. In 1983, he published *Frisson de bonheur* with Albin Michel; the following year, he joined forces with Jackie Berroyer to produce *Raoul Teigneux contre les Druzes* (Albin Michel), then with Professor Choron for the *Versets sataniques de l'Évangile*

(1989). Philippe Vuillemin shows us our faults, in exaggerated close-up, as in *Les Sales Blagues de l'Écho* (Albin Michel, 1987, thirteen volumes in total, of which the last was published in 2005), which would later be adapted for television. He succeeded Reiser in his column in *L'Écho des Savanes*. His cartoons are published in *Penthouse* and *Libération*, to whom he regularly lends his acid look at the world of work. A man of eclectic talents, he also acts (*Le Mystère Alexina*, 1985) and was the guitarist in the group Dennis' Twist, with Margerin and his friends. He won the Ville d'Angoulême prize in 1996.
Page: 114

## Philippe WEISBECKER

Born in 1942 in Dakar, Senegal, Philippe Weisbecker studied at the Charpentier Academy before joining the National School of Decorative Arts in Paris, from which he graduated in 1966. After his military service in Tunisia, he left for New York in 1968. There he was entranced by trucks, factories, antiquated tools and household utensils, which he drew in school exercise books with square paper. After being discovered by the American press, he published his illustrations made of collages based on leaflets, paper bags, fabric and mathematical notes. His love of popular culture, defence of the machine and geometrical drawings recall the Russian artists of the early 20th century. He came back to Paris in 1974, then left definitively for New York, where he taught at the prestigious School of Visuals Arts until 1983. His illustrations have been published in numerous magazines: *The Village Voice*, *Esquire*, *The New Yorker*, *Atlantic Monthly*, *The New York Times*, *Business Week*, *Enjeux les Échos*, *Forbes*, *Time Magazine*, *Le Monde* and *Vogue Japon*. He has illustrated several books – *Slash, an Alligator's Story* (Harlin Quist, 1971), *Goat Cheese* (Chronicle Books, 1997), *Précautions d'usage* (Être, 1998) and *Hand Tools* (Amus Arts Press, 2003) – but also annual reports, such as those of First Health in 2001, 2002 and 2004. His work has been exhibited all over the world: at the Louvre in Paris, in New York (from 1982 onward), in Venice, Tokyo, Osaka, Kyoto, Barcelona… Several American museums own Philippe Weisbecker illustrations.
Pages: 33, 174, 178

## Georges WOLINSKI

A comic book artist and writer born in Tunis in 1934, Georges Wolinski discovered comics through Dubout publications. He began his career in *Rustica*, in 1958, then in *Bizarre*, before joining the team at *Hara-Kiri* in 1960, alongside Cavanna and Professor Choron. He then became the editor of *Charlie*, where he stayed until 1981. In the meantime, he co-founded with Siné the magazine *L'Enragé*, in which he published his frank and militant cartoons – later collected in *Ma Voisine est une salope*, published in 1974. A press cartoonist for *L'Humanité*, *France-Soir*, *Libération*, *Télérama*, *Action*, *Paris-Presse*, *Le Nouvel Observateur*, *L'Écho des Savanes* and *Paris Match*, he was inspired by the news and bar-room politics. In these albums, Wolinski sketches our era: *Tu m'aimes?* (Albin Michel, 1985), *Scoopette. La nympho de l'info* (Canal + Éditions, 1994) and *Sacré Mitterrand!* (Albin Michel, 1996). With dozens of published works, compilations of news cartoons such as *Dialogues de sourds* (Le Cherche Midi, 2005), comic books such as the erotic adventures of *Paulette* drawn by Georges Pichard (the complete *Tout Paulette* was published by Albin Michel in 1998), numerous travel notebooks and advertising campaigns, Georges Wolinski is one of the most prolific writers and artists of his generation. He was awarded the main prize at the thirty-second Angoulême International Comics Festival in 2005. He is a *Chevalier* of the Legion of Honour.
Page: 111

## ACKNOWLEDGEMENTS

Thanks to Martine Parker-Landon who, since we created Vue sur la Ville, has helped to give concrete expression to my ideas
and bring my intentions to faithful and technologically inventive conclusions;
to Nicole Contencin, a very special partner, who always knows how to find the best sense and the right words;
to my editor Chantal Desmazières and her team, for their enthusiasm.

Thank you to the graphic designers, copywriters and technical staff, whose talent and knowledge
have contributed to the images and publications reproduced in this book:
Jacques Aubert, Françoise Aveline, Pascal Avot, Anne Barcat, Philippe Blanchard, Philippe Boiteux, Delphine Bommelaer, Muriel Bouret, Gwenaëlle Brochoire,
Fréderic Bortolotti, Eudes Bulard, Freddy Debbak, Christine Duchier-Lapeyre, Marion Félix, Annabelle Fournier, Jean-Luc Fromental, Vincent Giavelli,
Piera Grandesso, Rémi Joutet, François Landon, Julie Mattei, Agnès Muckensturm, Florence Osternaud, Magali Peretti, Jean-Pierre Révol, Hervé Rivoalland and Maïté Turonnet.

Thanks to those who, through their help and support, have made this book possible:
Philippe Arnaud, Isabelle Beaumenay, Peter Bertoux, Aimery Chemin, Virginie Challamel, Jean-Loup Chiflet, Marco De la Fuente, Julie Deydier,
Patrick Doucet, Guillaume Frauly, Sylvie Flaure, Thierry Gaugain, Jacques Helleu, Tiggy Maconochie, Séverine Merle, Guy Mestrallet, Ian Patrick,
Priska Peters, Jean-Marc Pias, Bérengère Ridoux, Valérie Schermann, François-Xavier Terny, Tiphaine, Francis Van Den Buch and Fréderic Verbrugghe.

Thanks to the advertising clients, who, through their trust and friendship, have allowed us to conceive and publish the illustrations and publications reproduced in this work:
Catherine Aurenche, Christian Bataille, Hélène Besnier, Patrick Charpentier, Marie-Louise de Clermont-Tonnerre, Corinne Delattre,
Claude Dimont-Mellac, Vincent Duhem, Valérie Duport, Françoise Flament, Marika Genty, Jean-Paul Goude, Marie Grandcolas, Solenn Gubri, Martine Guinot,
Francka Holtmann, Claudia Langer, Pierre Lescure, Sophie Melchior, Edith Morawetz, Dominique Montcourtois, Françoise Montenay, Sophie Montier-Leboucher,
Jean Poulallion, Isabelle Picard, Alexandra Rendall, Arielle Ricaud-Barsi, Dominik Rossler, Philippe Starck, Thierry Tuteleers, Denis Vergneau, Gilles Verlant, Gregor Woltje.

Thank you to all the artists whose works appear in this book, which I dedicate to them. A special mention for Yves Chaland.

Alain Lachartre

Les Éditions Scala express their gratitude to the advertisers and illustrators who have given their permission for the reproduction of these images.
They also thank their design team, Julie Mattei and Magali Peretti, their corrector Céline de Quéral, and Charlotte Barbe
their partners, Philippe Boiteux (Dupont Photogravure), Brigitte Legeay (Arjowiggins) and Pierre Le Govic (Imprimerie Le Govic)
as well as all those who, through their enthusiasm and participation, have made this publication possible.